George Napier of the 52nd

General Sir, George T. Napier K.C.B.

George Napier of the 52nd
Personal Recollections of Service With
the Light Division During the Peninsular War
Under Moore & Wellington

George T. Napier

George Napier of the 52nd
Personal Recollections of Service With
the Light Division During the Peninsular War Under Moore & Wellington
by George T. Napier

First published under the title
Passages in the Early Military Life of General Sir, George T. Napier K.C.B.

Leonaur is an imprint of Oakpast Ltd
Copyright in this form © 2012 Oakpast Ltd

ISBN: 978-0-85706-900-9 (hardcover)
ISBN: 978-0-85706-901-6 (softcover)

http://www.leonaur.com

Publisher's Notes

The views expressed in this book are not necessarily those of the publisher.

Contents

Preface	9
Choice of a Profession	11
Despatch of the Battle of Coruña	29
The Peninsular War	58
Advance from the Lines of Torres Vedras	84
Siege of Ciudad Rodrigo	104
Rejoin the 52nd at St. Jean de Luz	118
Sail for England	133
Concluding Extract	142
Appendix	146

DEDICATED
TO
THE 52ND LIGHT INFANTRY
IN WHICH GLORIOUS REGIMENT SIR GEORGE NAPIER
RECEIVED HIS EDUCATION AS A SOLDIER
AND PASSED THE HAPPIEST YEARS
OF HIS MILITARY CAREER

Preface

The narrative from which the following extracts are taken was written in the year 1828 by my father, entirely for the instruction and amusement of his children, and not with any view to publication. Having lately become possessed of the manuscript, it has appeared to me and to others of my family that the publication of portions of it might be useful to young officers, and not without interest to the general reader, as it relates to stirring times, and treats of scenes and men of historic interest and fame. I therefore venture to lay these extracts before the public, premising that if the language used and the lessons of morality and conduct inculcated appear to be simple and homely, it must be recollected that the narrative was written for boys and girls of a tender age.

General Sir George Thomas Napier was the second son of Colonel the Hon. George and Lady Sarah Napier. He was born in June 1784, entered the army in January 1800, at the age of fifteen and a half, served in the Coruña campaign as *aide-de-camp* to Sir John Moore, and in the Peninsular war with the 52nd Regiment; served afterwards in the Guards; was Governor of the Cape of Good Hope 1838-44, and died at Geneva on the 8th of September, 1855. What his character was will be gathered from the narrative itself.

CHAPTER 1

Choice of a Profession

I was at first determined to be a sailor, and was entered on the books of the *Invincible*, Captain Thomas Packenham; but as the sea disagreed with me I did not join the ship. I then thought I would be a clergyman (and a good clergyman, let me observe, is the most respectable of men; and if he has the will, has the power to do more real good to his fellow-creatures, and particularly to the poor, than almost any other member of society; there is no situation in which one can, by a scrupulous discharge of one's duty, prove more useful to mankind in this life, or more sure of being acceptable to God in the next), as my uncle, Mr. Conolly, had a living in Bedfordshire which he would have given me when fit for it.

However, after working at Latin I was so idle, and disliked it so much, that I would not go into the Church, but said I would be a soldier, as I liked fighting, a red coat, and a sword! Now here it is necessary to observe that it was lucky I was only a little boy at the time, and did not know my own mind, therefore, the saying I would change my profession was mere words and did not signify. Had I been a young man and entered first the navy, then altered my mind and gone to college to study for the Church, got tired of study, and after all entered the army, why, I should have been fit for nothing, being too old to like the drill and hard work a subaltern must go through; I should have acquired lazy and idle habits, and been totally unfit for my profession, which, above all others (except the navy), requires a man to be strong in body and mind, able and willing to bear fatigue, deprivations, and hardships of all kinds; and not only to bear them without a murmur, but to seek them, always volunteering for every sort of duty; for the greater the fatigue, the more severe the hardships, and greater the danger, the more glorious is the soldier's life. When a man once fixes on a profession he is bound to pursue it ardently, zealously, and indefatigably, till he mounts to the top of it, or is provided for by death.

Now to resume my narrative. Being, as I said, determined to enter the army, I studied, or rather flattered myself I studied, mathematics and French, but not being much looked after, what I did learn was very superficial, and I soon forgot it all, to my inexpressible sorrow, as even the little I did acquire would now be of vast use to you [his children]. Your uncle Charles, on the contrary, being very clever, persevering, and of a studious turn of mind, learned so well and so thoroughly, that he soon got over all difficulties, and made himself master of the theoretical part of his profession by the time he was a captain, and was appointed to a regiment called the 'Staff Corps,' which only such officers as are good mathematicians, understand fortification, military drawing, and are fit for the staff of the army, are allowed to enter, and it is a great feather in a young officer's cap to get a commission in that distinguished regiment.

There he studied still harder, and has, in consequence of his attention to the study of his profession, distinguished himself as an officer in a double ratio to me; not that I mean to say, even if I had studied, I should ever have been so skilful an officer as your Uncle Charles, not being by nature so clever a man, but I should have been a much better officer than I am. Your Uncle William, being fond of reading and studying his profession in various ways, and also a very clever man, gifted by nature with great abilities and much talent, has, by his excellent history of the war in Spain, gained as much honour and celebrity as a writer as he has reaped glory as a soldier. Thus you have two excellent examples in your own family, in the profession you mean to enter, of what study and application may accomplish.

Had any of you determined to enter the navy (which I am sorry you have not) I should have pointed out your Uncle Henry as an example, for, although he has not got on as well as he deserves, he is considered as a most excellent, skilful, and deserving officer by his own profession, and has studied it perhaps with more zeal and ability than most men. But in the navy, I am sorry to say, merit is seldom rewarded in proportion to its deserts; but now that His Royal Highness the Duke of Clarence is placed at the head of that service, which is the safeguard and bulwark of England, and ought to be cherished beyond all others, I have no doubt that justice will be done to every member and branch of it. But I must proceed with my narrative, or you will think me as dull and tedious as our parish parson.

Lord Cornwallis, who was one of the best soldiers and most excellent, humane, high-minded, honourable, and virtuous men that ever graced the annals of English history, being an old and long tried friend of my father and mother, gave me a cornetcy of dragoons on January 1, 1800, I being then fifteen years and a half old; and no boy of that age, or any age, I will venture to say, ever felt greater delight than I did on reading in the *Gazette*, 'George Thomas Napier, gent., to be cornet in the 24th Light Dragoons.' A very few days were necessary to get my uniform made, as I worried the tailor's life out till it was done, and never shall I forget the excitement with which I read on my helmet the motto '*Death or Glory*.' My dear mother, with tears in her eyes, half joy, half sorrow, placed it on my head, and from that moment I made an inward vow that '*Death or Glory*' should be my watchword in the hour of battle; and I am vain enough to say, throughout a life of nearly thirty years' service it has never failed me; and much as I love you all, my dear children, much as it would grieve me to leave you and your dear aunt whenever the 'shout of war' is heard and my duty to my country calls me, I shall go again to seek '*Death or Glory*' in her sacred cause.

Great as is my duty towards you, and bound as I am by every tie of nature to perform it; however great the personal and family sacrifices I must make, still a *soldier's* first and paramount duty is to his country. All private benefit, all feelings, all affections, in short, life itself, must yield to that; and I solemnly warn you, my dear boys, before you enter the army to bear in mind and clearly to understand that once having done so you are bound to endure every sacrifice that duty calls upon you to make; and that strong as my paternal affection is, and it is as deep as any father's can be, I would spurn you from me if ever you suffered any motive whatever to keep you from the performance of your duty to your King and country! Nay, I would rather, far rather, see your bloody corpses shrouded in a soldier's cloak than hear you taunted with having failed in the performance of your duty as soldiers! Nothing, nothing but bad health can ever excuse a man of honour (and without honour life's a burthen) from a complete, full, and zealous discharge of his duty.

I have dwelt upon this subject because I know the neglect of it has been the ruin and misery of many a good man; and I conscientiously feel I owe what little credit I may have gained as an officer to my constant determination never to shrink from the performance of any duty however disagreeable to mind or body (and in a soldier's life he must have many such duties), but to pursue my profession with unabated zeal.

As soon as I had got all my things and bought some horses I joined my regiment in Dublin barracks, and you will easily imagine what a happy fellow I was to be my own master at fifteen, with a fine uniform, a couple of horses, a servant, and about fifty pounds in my pocket. This certainly was one of the happiest periods of my life, and little did I then think I was destined to be an actor in, and witness, so many extraordinary events as have taken place during the last thirty years!

In the dragoons I remained only six months, where, I must acknowledge, however painful the confession, that except to ride and get a tolerable knowledge of horses, paying well in my purse for the same, I learned nothing but to drink, [1] and enter into every kind of debauchery, which is disreputable to a gentleman. Such conduct, thank God, is now, and has been for many years, given up by the officers of the army, and it is considered as most ungentlemanlike, vulgar, and disgraceful to be drunk or even tipsy. As to gaming, I warn you against it as the most dreadful of all vices; it corrupts the heart, debases the mind, destroys the temper, and ruins the prospects of every unfortunate wretch who is caught in its snares.

My father, being an old soldier, was convinced I should go to ruin if I remained any longer in the dragoons, and, therefore, procured me a lieutenancy in the 46th Regiment of Foot, then quartered in Limerick, in the south of Ireland, famous for its beautiful women, and deservedly so, for I never saw such a number of pretty girls collected in one town before or since. The general commanding the district was an old and most intimate friend of my father's (Sir James Duff), to whom your Uncle Charles was at the time *aide-de-camp*, so that on joining the 46th Regiment in June 1800, I was under Sir James's eye, and also my brother's, who, as I told you, was a very steady fellow, and never drank any wine, or committed follies of any kind.

I did not much like giving up my horses and going into the infantry, but having very high spirits and robust health, the novelty of going a distance from home and being promoted to a lieutenancy soon reconciled me to my new regiment, which, although with the reputation of being a very good one, had the faults of most regiments at that time, namely, much quarrelling among the officers and

---

1. My father afterwards gave up all liquor, and became the most abstemious of men.—Ed. (W.N.).

drinking to excess; therefore I did not benefit much by the change of regiments, but I did profit by living a great deal with Sir James and Lady Duff, to whom I am most grateful for all the parental kindness I received from them. From Sir James I learned that although a man was wild, and drank as our officers did, yet if he was an honourable man, and had the feelings of a gentleman, he never would, even in his drunken moments, do a cowardly or unmanly act. From Lady Duff I learned good manners, and observed from her conduct and character how superior a woman of sense was to all the follies of the fashionable and giddy world. And let me here remark that it is the duty of every man, and more particularly a soldier, to show every attention, civility, and kindness to the female sex, and to be ever prompt to protect them from insult or impertinence.

About six months after I joined the 46th, Sir James Duff was made a lieutenant-general, and my brother Charles having gone to join the rifle corps, I was appointed, with Lady Duff's nephew, James Douglas (now Major-General Sir James Douglas), to be one of his *aides-de-camp*. I remained very happy in that situation till the year 1802, when Sir James Duff was removed from the staff, and my battalion being also reduced in consequence of the Peace of Amiens, I was placed on half-pay, and went to England for a few weeks.

On my return to Ireland I was appointed to the 52nd Regiment of Light Infantry, which was Sir John Moore's, and commanded by Colonel MacKenzie. And now I come to that period of my life from whence I may date the commencement of my military career, as till I entered the 52nd Regiment I had learned nothing of my profession. I had nearly forgotten to tell you that, while at Limerick with your Uncle Charles, going out one day to shoot snipes, he, your uncle, shot one, and springing over a deep ditch in order to get it, he fell and broke his leg, which gave a crack like a whip. Upon my running up to him he laughed, and called out to me, 'Though I have broken my leg, I've got the snipe!'

The 52nd Regiment was quartered at Chatham, under the immediate command of Sir John Moore, and when I called upon him to pay my respects upon joining, he received me very kindly, turned me round, looked at me, and then laughingly said, 'Oh, you will do; I see you are a good cut of a light infantryman,—come and dine with me.' This was my first introduction to that great and good soldier. From that time he treated me like a son. I never was from under his command, and I am proud, most proud, to say I never received the slightest reproof from his lips, was with him through all his subsequent difficulties and sufferings till that dreadful night when I saw him to whom I looked up as the first of men, a bloody corpse, without the melancholy satisfaction of hearing his last heroic words, '*I hope the people of England will be satisfied*,' addressed to that country which he loved with an ardour equal to the Roman patriot's, and had served to the hour of his death with a zeal and gallantry equalled by few, surpassed by none.

Very soon Colonel Kenneth MacKenzie took the command of the regiment, to which Sir John Moore had him appointed as the officer at that period best adapted to form a Light Infantry regiment, ours being the first of that description of force; and as Colonel MacKenzie was an old, experienced, and skilful officer, and had served a great deal, and particularly distinguished himself in Egypt in command of the 90th Regiment, and, indeed, was generally considered the best commanding officer in the army, Sir John Moore was fully justified in his choice of such an officer to command his regiment, of which he was proud to the greatest degree, and loved and treated us all as if we were his children. It was impossible for any father to devote himself more to the welfare of his sons than did Sir John Moore to that of his officers, and no parent could be more revered and beloved than he was by us all—officers, non-commissioned officers, and privates.

Colonel MacKenzie began by assembling the officers and telling them that the only way of having a regiment in good order was by every individual thoroughly knowing and performing his duty; and that if the officers did not fully understand their duty, it would be quite impossible to expect that the men either could or would perform theirs as they ought; therefore the best and surest method was to commence by drilling the whole of the officers, and when they became perfectly acquainted with the system, they could teach the men, and by their zeal, knowledge, and, above all, good temper and kind treatment of the soldier, make the regiment the best in the service; and, as he predicted, it did become the finest and best behaved corps, both as regarded officers and men, that ever was seen; and by the system then commenced and afterwards perfected, the 52nd Regiment was considered as a model for the rest of the army, and was the *nucleus* from which that beautiful brigade, consisting of the 43rd, 52nd, and Rifle Corps, was formed at Shorncliffe camp under Sir John Moore's own eye, and which afterwards was so distinguished in the Peninsular War as *The Light Division* of the Duke of Wellington's army under General Robert Craufurd, and which gave commanding officers to many a regiment in that army, as well as numerous adjutants and subalterns chosen from the *non-commissioned* officers of those three regiments.

The great thing that Sir John Moore and Colonel MacKenzie used to impress upon the minds of the officers was that our duty was to do everything in our power to *prevent* crime, as then there would be no occasion for punishment; and if any of you, my sons, obtain the command of a regiment, recollect that it is by the unfrequency of crimes in your regiment, and not by the few punishments that may appear in the regimental books, that a general officer will judge of its state of discipline and of your capacity and conduct as a commanding officer.

We marched from Chatham to Canterbury, but before I left Chatham I was made very unhappy by hearing of the death of my uncle, Mr. Conolly, of Castletown, to whose kindness I owed so much, and who was the best and greatest friend your uncles, your aunts, and myself ever had. He was a great loss to Ireland, for no man was ever more devotedly attached to his country, or had exerted himself more zealously in every way, publicly and privately, for the prosperity and honour of Ireland from first to last. He had a sound, clear judgement without being a man of talent; was a man of rigid integrity and high honour, of an open, frank, and superbly generous disposition, caring for money only as it gave the means of making others happy and comfortable.

As he was perfectly free from guile or deceit himself, so he never suspected others of those truly detestable vices, and was consequently often cheated and the dupe of designing men, so far as giving money to those who were unworthy of his generosity; but no man, however cunning or deceitful, could work on him to do a dishonourable or mean act; the instant they attempted it he saw through them, and would spurn them from him with the contempt they deserved.

During the time we were quartered at Canterbury, having been extravagant and got into debt with the paymaster of the regiment, two other young officers, who, like myself, were in debt, agreed that, as it was very uncomfortable and disreputable to owe money, we would no longer live at the mess, but be content to live in our own lodgings upon plain bread and milk till we should be able to pay off our debts; and it was three months before we again joined the mess. The two officers, my companions in this, were brothers—Robert and Charles Rowan; the former has since left the army, and the latter is now Colonel Rowan,[2] and the head of the police establishment in London.

---

2. Colonel Charles Rowan served in the Peninsula, France, and Flanders; was wounded at Waterloo.

Now there is nothing so disadvantageous or disagreeable, particularly to a young officer, as being obliged to leave the mess of his regiment, as it is, or *ought to be*, so regulated that if he is not an extravagant and careless fellow, and conducts himself like a gentleman, he can always live with his brother-officers and enjoy their society. If he quits the mess he is in disgrace, but then it is better to acknowledge and be punished for his errors by being very uncomfortable for a few months, as we were, than to find himself so involved in difficulties and debt that he is obliged to leave the army.

We marched from Canterbury to Hythe on the coast of Kent, and remained in that neighbourhood for about three years, as the French (war having been declared) had assembled a large force in the camp of Boulogne, on the opposite coast, and Napoleon Buonaparte threatened to invade England with this immense army; and for a long time he kept the whole English nation and the Ministry of the time (Mr. Pitt at its head) in a continual dread. The whole male population of England was armed—at least, all those who were capable of using arms—and organised in corps of cavalry and infantry, and the regular and militia force was ready to move at a moment's warning to any particular spot where Napoleon might land, or attempt to land. There would have been collected at Shorncliffe, and along that coast from Deal to Hastings, in a few hours no less than 40,000 excellent troops to oppose the enemy, principally under Sir John Moore, in whom Mr. Pitt had the most unbounded confidence as an officer; and, in case of this first line being obliged to fall back, there was another line ready to support the first of 50,000 troops, besides large bodies of armed peasantry, all breathing defiance and rage against the French; and I am convinced, from all I have since seen and known of the French troops, that had Napoleon effected a landing, he *never* could have reached London! his army would have been destroyed, and few would have returned to tell the tale!

Moreover, I think Napoleon had no intention of making the attempt, although I am not borne out in that opinion by one of the greatest of his marshals, Marshal Soult, who was with Napoleon in that army at Boulogne, and who told me he really thought Napoleon did mean to try it.[3] Other French generals, who were conversing with the marshal at the same time, were of a different opinion, and *not one* seemed to be confident of success; even Marshal Soult, when I asked him what he thought of that part, replied: '*Eh! monsieur, c'est une autre*

---

3. I believe there is now no doubt that such was Napoleon's intention.—Ed. (W.N.)

affaire,' and the conversation finished. Now I infer from that expression that my friend, Marshal Soult, was not quite so confident of success as his great master Napoleon, and I verily believe that after Napoleon had seen what British troops were capable of at Waterloo he altered his opinion also.

About this time, January 1804, I purchased a company in the regiment over the heads of many lieutenants, by which I got a great advance in my profession. I had been four years a subaltern, and was nineteen years and a half old, which was very young to be a captain. At the time the company became vacant, I could not get the money to buy it, and was very sorry to be obliged to give up all idea of it, when an intimate friend of mine, a captain in the regiment, and whose subaltern I was, without saying a word to me, went off to London and lodged the 950*l.* (the regulation price) in the agent's hands upon my account, and I was immediately gazetted as captain. This friend was Lord Frederick Bentinck, who, after having served his country for thirty years and upwards with great credit, and arrived at the rank of major-general and colonel of the 58th Regiment, died a few months ago (1828) at Rome, of consumption.

I must not pass over my beloved and lamented friend Lord Frederick's death without informing you that he was my earliest friend, and one whom I loved with all a brother's affection. He was a couple of years older than myself, but from the time I was fifteen to the hour of his death, I may say we were in habits of intimacy, and a more generous, guileless, warmhearted, single-minded man never breathed. His purse and heart were open to all who were worthy of so good and excellent a man's kindness; he was brave as ever man was; and, although not a brilliant officer, had seen so much service, and had such good sense, that he made up by experience and zeal for the want of more shining abilities. He commanded the advanced guard under his brother, Lord William Bentinck, in Catalonia, and, as long as it was under his orders, everything went on well.

Not so afterwards, when he was superseded by Sir Frederick Adam, who had the reputation of being a great genius; but sometimes your great geniuses get into scrapes which ordinary men would have kept out of. Lord Frederick fought, and, I think, took prisoner, the French general of cavalry in single combat, sword in hand. I was enabled to pay him back the money he lent me to purchase my company some years afterwards, but, had I not done so, it would have been all the same to Frederick Bentinck, for he never would have asked me; on the contrary, often did he wish me to accept the money as a proof of friendship.

In the autumn of 1804, my brother William, who was in the Blues, exchanged into the 52nd, and was my lieutenant. Sir John Moore, who was fond of William, very soon got him a company for nothing, and had him appointed to the 43rd Light Infantry, in which regiment he remained till the year 1818. The officers of the 43rd, in which he had served so long, and which he had often commanded in most of the battles in Spain, were very sorry to lose him, and, as a mark of their affection and esteem, made him a present of a very magnificent sword.

Soon after I was a captain I was sent to get volunteers from a militia regiment in Ireland, and your Uncle William was also sent from his regiment for the same purpose, so we went off together to Limerick. One day there came to your uncle and me ten very handsome militia soldiers, six feet high, who said they would volunteer with whichever officer of the line (for there were a number of us all on the same duty) could beat them in running and jumping. Of course, in order to get these fine fellows, we all tried and exerted ourselves to the utmost. Your uncle and I were the two most active of all the officers, and we had a hard struggle with Pat; but I was beat by them. Not so your uncle; with his cursed long legs he beat the men both in running and jumping, and they, being . honourable fellows, as most Irishmen are, kept their word, and he took them all ten to the 43rd, and probably most of them found their graves in Spain, poor fellows!

We returned to our regiments, and I was immediately sent off to Guernsey on the same duty, and afterwards to the Isle of Wight, where there was a reserve battalion from which Sir John Moore expected to get a great number of men for the 52nd, as it was commanded by one of the finest fellows and best officers in the service, who, he knew, would do all in his power to make the men volunteer. So he did, for I got an immense number. The officer I allude to was then Lieut.-Colonel Samuel Gibbs (afterwards a general and Knight of the Bath), who had highly distinguished himself in India, and was killed as second in command to Sir Edward Pakenham at New Orleans, in America. Had he lived he would have been considered, and indeed was, one of our very first officers.

The number of volunteers we got was so great that a second battalion was given to the regiment; and in consequence of its being in such high order, and at the recommendation of the general, all the promotion was allowed to go in the regiment. At the same time the king (George III.) made General Moore a Knight of the Bath, at that time only given to such *general officers* as had particularly distinguished themselves on service. Upon this occasion the officers of the 52nd subscribed a large sum of money and bought a beautiful diamond star, which they presented to Sir John Moore as a mark of their esteem and affection. The star was worth five or six hundred guineas, I forget which. Sir John Moore was highly pleased and gratified with this proof of the respect, esteem, love, and gratitude of his officers, and well did he deserve every proof in our power to give, for never did any colonel of a regiment pay such attention to the happiness and interests of his regiment as he did to the hour of his death. But that which gratified him most was the good conduct and zeal of both officers and men in the performance of their duty, and often would he tell us he felt prouder of having such a regiment than he did of his red ribbon.

In this year, 1804, my father died. He had been long ill of a consumptive complaint, and the indefatigable zeal with which he attended to the business of his office in Dublin made the confinement too much for the weak state of his health. He was ordered by the physicians to go to Clifton, near Bristol, where in a few weeks he breathed his last. My father had a beautiful figure, and was six feet two inches in height, with one of the handsomest faces I ever saw, and was the most perfect-made man possible. He was in his younger days looked upon as the most active and the handsomest officer of the British Army in America, where he was serving with his regiment as a captain against the Americans, who had separated themselves from the mother country. As well as being so fine a looking man, he was as clever and able in mind as strong in body.

There were few things that he did not succeed in: he had read a great deal in many languages, was a good classic scholar, well acquainted with all history, ancient and modern, was a good mathematician, engineer, and chemist, and had written several papers and reports upon these latter subjects when he was controller of the Laboratory at Woolwich; he was an excellent regimental officer, and had served through all the American War, and was deputy quarter master-general to the army commanded by the Marquis of Hastings, which went to Holland in the year 1794, after which he commanded the Londonderry Regiment.

When placed upon half-pay in consequence of his regiment being drafted into regiments in the West Indies, he was made Controller of

Army Accounts in Ireland by his friend Lord Cornwallis, then lord-lieutenant, by whose humanity, skill, and judgement in governing Ireland the rebellion in that unhappy country was put an end to; at the same time the horrid cruelties practised with so much barbarity were effectually put a stop to, and while Lord Cornwallis was at the head of that oppressed country, justice was administered impartially to the poor peasant and degraded Catholics.

In the year 1806, Sir John Moore was appointed second in command in Sicily, under General Fox. In a few weeks the 52nd followed him under the command of Major-General Paget, accompanied by the Guards and several other regiments. We embarked at Deal, and had a boisterous passage down Channel and in the Bay of Biscay; many of the men-of-war being disabled in the gales, several transports with horses were lost, and others driven on the French coast and taken prisoners. One unfortunate transport with horses on board was run down by a large ship, which passed clean over her, and not a vestige of her was ever seen again. The ship I was on board of was run foul of by a frigate, but being a very fine new large vessel she suffered comparatively little damage. I was so sick that notwithstanding everyone thought we were sinking, and all hands were trying to escape into the shrouds of the frigate, I could not move, but resigned myself to my fate without the least effort; such is the powerful effect of seasickness on the mind as well as body.

In a few days the weather cleared up, and on a fine bright morning, the anniversary of the glorious Battle of Trafalgar, on the very spot where that greatest of all naval battles was fought the year before, in which the immortal Nelson fell, as he had lived, the pride of England's navy and the successful conqueror and destroyer of the fleets of France, did we meet that *same British fleet* under the command of that excellent, skilful, gallant, and good man Lord Collingwood. Immediately the signal was made by our commander, Sir Thomas Duckworth, for the ships of the convoy to pass under the admiral's stern; the soldiers dressed and paraded on the decks, with bands playing 'Rule Britannia' and colours flying; and as we passed our colours dropped, and, presenting arms, we gave three hearty cheers, the fine sailor-like old admiral taking off his hat and bowing to us, his own brave crew and the rest of his fleet returning our cheers with loud huzzahs.

My ship, in which was our band, was, curiously enough, called the *Collingwood* after him, and had a fine large figure of the admiral at her head, painted in full uniform, and we led the van in this well-merited compliment as Collingwood himself had led the van in the battle. I never felt more elated or saw a finer sight!

From thence we proceeded to the Straits of Gibraltar, and on our arrival in the Bay of Tangier, on a beautiful fine evening, we were ordered by signal from Sir T. Duckworth to 'lay to' till next morning, as he feared the Spanish gunboats would come out as we entered the Straits and snap some of us up. Unfortunately for us, during the night a *levanter* (so called from the wind blowing from the Levant down the Mediterranean) came with such force that the fleet was dispersed and driven away to the Atlantic. My ship was twenty-two days cruising off Cape Spartel, on the north-west coast of Africa, before the wind changed and enabled us to bear up and sail through the Straits and anchor in the Bay of Tetuan (on the African coast, just opposite Gibraltar), where we were to take in fresh meat and water. The poor cattle were bought by the commissaries at the town of Tetuan from the Moors, and then brought alongside the ships in boats, where a rope being fastened round their horns, they were hoisted on board by a pulley, which is very cruel, for I have often seen the horns completely dragged out of the head and the wretched bullock drop into the boat again writhing with agony.

While at Tetuan, being one day on shore with a watering party, the Moorish captain or chief of the guard placed there to prevent the English soldiers from going into the town asked me in English (for he could speak it a little) to give him some brandy, which I very foolishly did, and he got intoxicated; and having given some also to several of his men, the consequence was that our soldiers and the Moors began to quarrel, and it ended in a general fight, the English, of course, soon beating off the Moors. Then came down a strong reinforcement from the town, with several officers sent by the governor with orders to make us all prisoners. Of course this we would not submit to for the Emperor of Morocco himself if he had been there in person, but I told the chief in command I would return on board ship again with my party, and he might report the circumstance to the English general; but as to making myself or any of my people prisoners, that he should not do as long as I had command of them, and I immediately drew them up ready to fire upon him if he presumed to attempt any violence.

He was very angry and blustered about, but seeing there was no use in trying force, he wisely contented himself with brandishing his sabre, making his men prance their horses, and gallop about very actively, for they were all beautifully mounted on barbs, and taking hold of the poor drunken officer said he should have his head cut off immediately for being drunk and neglecting his duty; accordingly they tied the poor devil neck and heels, and throwing him across a horse away they galloped to the town, where the poor fellow was degraded as an officer but not put to death, only well bastinadoed. You see, by my being so foolish as to give him drink, he nearly lost his life, was cashiered as an officer, and severely flogged, besides the risk of a fight between the Moors and my men, in which most probably many lives would have been lost, and all caused by my imprudence and want of forethought.

I mention this little anecdote in order to impress on your minds the necessity of always reflecting upon what you are about to do, otherwise, more particularly as officers, you will often be in some scrape which a very little reflection would have prevented. An officer should never go on any duty, however insignificant it may appear to him, but in the full determination of considering well in his own mind what will be the best way of performing that duty in the quickest and most efficient manner, and with the least possible risk of the safety of those placed under his command, never forgetting that upon his conduct and judgement may depend the lives of hundreds, and that no precaution should be neglected consistent with the duty he is sent to perform; then, if unfortunately he should fail, it will most probably not be his fault; and, much as every man must regret failure, it is a great consolation to feel he is conscious of having used every means and made every effort that was in his power to ensure success.

After having completed our water in Tetuan Bay (which, by-theby, is a beautiful situation, with a magnificent view of the mountains which frown over the town and the strong fort of Ceuta, which belongs to the Spaniards, and of which they are very jealous, as it commands the Straits on the African sides, and is in time of war a great annoyance to our merchant vessels when becalmed, which often happens, and then the Spanish gunboats move out under cover of the guns of the fort and whip up our merchantmen at a great rate) we proceeded 'aloft' (the term used for going up the Mediterranean Sea), and in about six weeks we arrived at Messina, in Sicily. It was a brilliant day, and I was much struck with the beauty of the coast on both sides of the Straits.

The current is so rapid, and there are so many eddies and whirlpools, that although I thought we were near enough to chuck a biscuit on shore, it was many hours before we were able to cast anchor, for just as we thought ourselves safe in harbour, in one minute an eddy carried us off to the opposite side of the Straits, where, on the Calabrian shore, there is a rock called 'Scylla,' so that if you escape the whirlpool of 'Charybdis,' on the Sicilian shore, you are driven against the rock of Scylla. Messina is a very beautiful old town, full of ancient ruins caused by earthquakes, which have so frequently taken place there that there are many streets in ruins.

Our regiment was ordered to go round the island by sea to a town called Melazzo, situated on a promontory, where we remained the whole time we were in Sicily. Nearly all the officers were permitted to go and see Mount Etna except myself. I did not get leave, having consented to take other officers' duty to let them go, and by that means I was delayed so long that the *very day* General Paget and I were preparing to go off to Etna, an order came for us to embark on a secret expedition, and so there was an end to my hopes of seeing Mount Etna, as well as various other curious places and things, which was very vexatious; and I strongly advise you boys never to miss seeing everything you possibly can wherever you may be quartered.

First do your duty and then make arrangements with your brother officers, so as to enable you to get leave for a short time to travel about, gaining all the information in your power relative to the customs, manners, habits, laws, productions, and population of the country you are in, as well as the means of subsistence for an army and the inhabitants themselves; in a word, everything in the way of information, as it will some time or other be of use to you; but the first thing an officer should do upon entering a new country is to make himself master of the language, as that is the thing of all others the most useful. You should never march through a country or travel anywhere without well and carefully observing the nature of the ground in a military point of view: for instance, the heights that command the road on which an army may be *en route*; what number of rivers you cross; if they have bridges; and if not, whether the fords are easy of passage for infantry, cavalry, or artillery; whether the banks are steep or level with the water; if mountain streams or rapid broad rivers; what provisions the country produces; whether it is a corn or a grazing country; the means of carriage, whether by horses, mules, or waggons.

Never forget the names of the towns and villages, and distances between each; the number of houses, as well as you can guess or get information of; the reputed number of inhabitants of each place, as well as the population in a lump of the whole country; what is the principal commerce carried on in every considerable town, as by that you may have an idea of the wealth of the people and judge what they can afford to be taxed, or, in military parlance, what amount of contribution might be justly levied upon them for the subsistence of the troops, supposing you to be in an enemy's country.

You should keep a journal in order to be accurate in your information when called upon; and it is always in an officer's power to do so, as you need only have a pocket-book with a clasp and pencil, which you can carry in your breast-pocket, ready to write a short note of whatever strikes you, with date and name of the place, and afterwards, when you have more time, and your baggage comes up, write at length in your regular journal, which should be of a good size, bound, with lines and a broad margin, in order to make notes at any future period when circumstances may come to your recollection which you may wish to mark particularly.

During the time we remained in Sicily wine was so cheap and plentiful and our soldiers drank so hard that great numbers were in hospital, and many died; but, what is worse, many of the men in their drunken fits killed their comrades, and were accordingly hung for murder, as it would never do to let drunkenness be an excuse for murder. I was on several courts-martial which sentenced the prisoners to be hung, and although I very much disliked sentencing a fellow-creature to death, still it was my duty to do so; but it leaves a very painful sensation on the mind for a long time after. Many young officers when members of a court-martial, being tired with sitting several hours, begin to amuse themselves with cutting pens or the table, or scribbling upon paper to pass away the time.

Now all this is very wrong and highly improper, as it is utterly impossible for those officers either to do their duty to the king or the prisoner, as it requires the strictest attention to all the evidence—pro and con—in order to make up your mind on the justice of the sentence you are going to pronounce, and which is to be inflicted on a fellow-creature. An officer should never forget that being a member of a court-martial is one of the most solemn duties he has to perform, and while performing that duty he should permit nothing else to engage his attention, but devote his whole mind and thoughts to the impartial performance of it, and then, what-ever may be the result, his conscience will not reproach him with having been guilty of any neglect.

While in Sicily, I was once detached from headquarters to a place in the hills called Gisso, where one day an orderly dragoon arrived and delivered to me the following letter from Sir John Moore:—

Messina, July 15, 1807.

My dear Napier,—Some people of rather a suspicious description have been reported to have been seen about the mountains over this. They are dressed and armed like the masses of Calabria. Among them are Frenchmen who have spy-glasses, and are said to have been seen sketching. It is possible they may pass through or take up their lodgings at night at Gisso or in the village below. It would be well to give orders, if any people of this description are seen in your neighbourhood, that quietly you may be informed of it, and then by calling on the magistrate you would find if he knew them. If he did not, and they could not give an account of themselves, they should ,be arrested and reported, or sent to headquarters. You are aware how much discretion must be used in obtaining this sort of information so as not to give alarm to those we wish to take, nor to molest others who have no concern with it; but I feel I risk nothing in giving you this information, which will tend to excite your vigilance without tempting you to act unless you see good cause. Believe me

Sincerely yours,

John Moore.

Immediately upon the receipt of this letter I disguised myself as a peasant, and taking my compass and map with me, as well as my spy-glass, I started into the mountains, with a gun on my shoulder and a pair of pistols under my waistcoat, and made a tour round my own immediate neighbourhood; and although I did not meet any of these people, I gained sufficient information to have an idea where they were, and that there was a considerable number of them. This information I forthwith transmitted to Sir John Moore, and received the following letter in answer:—

My dear Napier,—Many thanks to you for your letter and for the activity you have shown on the subject about which I wrote to you. I only beg that you will not allow your zeal to carry you so far as to risk yourself by putting yourself in the power of any vagabonds should you fall in with them. They should be traced, and then a strong body of soldiers sent to seize them in the night. General Oakes is also employing people to make the same discovery. I shall perhaps see you in a day or two on my passage to Palermo.

                    Sincerely yours

                                John Moore.

Immediately after this letter came an order from the quartermaster-general, directing me to proceed, according to a route sent with the order, to a certain place in the mountains with one hundred men and the necessary number of officers, where I should meet and join detachments from the Guards and other regiments sent from different parts of the island on the same service. I put myself and party accordingly *en route* at nine at night, and marched for many hours over the worst road I ever saw before or since, till we came to a very curious old walled town on the summit of a high mountain, which we passed through without waking the inhabitants, after well examining the town and satisfying myself that none of the people we were in search of were in it.

At last, after a harassing night march, we saw, at 11 o'clock a.m., the other detachments in the valley below us, not one of them having seen or heard anything of the objects of our pursuit, so we marched home again. The whole thing turned out to be that a body of poor Calabrese peasants had passed over from the opposite shore, bringing their arms with them, and were proceeding to Palermo to see the king, and to beg to be allowed to enter the Sicilian army, as they had not the means of subsistence in Calabria. Thus closed my first campaign, which I only relate to show you that I got approbation from Sir John Moore because I was active and zealous, and to induce you to do the same whenever you are employed on service of any kind.

Soon after this we embarked for England, and, touching at Gibraltar, where we remained for a fortnight, we landed at Portsmouth; but in less than three months we again embarked and sailed for Gottenburg, in Sweden.

CHAPTER 2

Despatch of the Battle of Coruña

We remained at anchor at Gottenburg for several weeks, while Sir John Moore, whose army was about 10,000 men, went to see the king at Stockholm, to consult with him as to the operations of the force under his orders; but, finding Gustavus to be full of wild impracticable schemes, and that he would not listen to reason, and required him to place the British Army under his command, in order to divide it into different parts and place it under the orders of his own generals, Sir John Moore refused to co-operate with him, and manfully told his Majesty that he was sent to Sweden by the King of England, his master, and the command of the British Army intrusted to him; that he was ready to act in concert with the Swedish Army, and to undertake anything that was feasible; but that he neither could nor would run the risk of having that army destroyed in attempting what was impracticable, and that, seeing he could be of no use, he should immediately carry the troops home again; and, finally, that his master had given him the command, and that to him alone would he deliver it up.

Upon this Gustavus flew into a violent rage, put Sir John Moore under arrest with a sentinel at his door, and swore he would take command of the British army in spite of him. Sir John Moore, knowing that he had a madman to deal with, made his escape during the night in the dress of a peasant; and one day a number of us were on board the *Victory*, Sir James Saumarez's flagship, at a ball given by the officers of that ship (which was the one in which Lord Nelson was killed at Trafalgar) to the Swedish ladies of Gottenburg, when a fishing-boat came alongside, and a peasant ran up the side and sprang on the quarter-deck! All the officers looked astonished, and wondered who the devil that impudent fellow was, when I looked at him and instantly recognised the general! He laughed, and, taking off his peasant's cap, asked the admiral if he did not know him.

Of course we were all delighted to see him back, as we had heard a rumour of something having gone wrong. Had he not been able to get away, I believe it was the intention of the admiral and Sir John Hope, the second in command, to have sailed round to Stockholm and demanded his release forthwith. Colonel Colborne, who had accompanied him, was left there for some time, and joined us at sea on our way back to England, as we sailed the day after Sir John Moore came on board the *Victory*. Upon arriving at Portsmouth, Sir John went up to London to give an account of this foolish *wild-goose chase*, for it was nothing else; and we were only sent to Sweden to get Sir John Moore out of the way, and serve a political intrigue of Mr. Canning and Lord Castlereagh! That's the fact, and deny it they never could; and, as Sir John Moore boldly and fearlessly told Lord Castlereagh what he thought of his conduct, he made him his enemy for life; though I must do Lord Castlereagh the justice to believe that he was kept up in his anger and dislike of Sir John Moore by interested people, who never failed to give a wrong construction to everything the general said or wrote, and, above all, by Canning.

In about ten days after we came to anchor at Spithead, we got orders to sail again, Sir John Moore being superseded in the command by Sir Harry Burrard, whom Lord Castlereagh sent down from London to take charge of the army, Sir John Moore remaining as second in command, which was not at all what the ministers wanted, for they expected that General Moore would not serve as second. But they little knew the man they had to deal with, for he never would be deterred from giving the benefit of his talents and experience to his country by any insult of any intriguing ministry; and so, to their dismay, he went with the army to Portugal, where we arrived too late to take part in the Battle of Vimiera, which the Duke of Wellington, then Sir Arthur Wellesley, had fought the day before we arrived, and in which he had beaten the French Army commanded by General Junot.

The consequence of this battle was that the French entered into a treaty with the British commander-in-chief. Sir Hugh Dalrymple, who had arrived from Gibraltar, by which the French troops were permitted to embark on board British ships with their arms and baggage, and were to be landed at a French port as soon as possible. This convention was loudly and *ignorantly* decried as cowardly and disgraceful to the British Army, and this shameful and most unjust outcry was supported and encouraged by the ministry; whereas, nothing could be more useful to the great object of sending troops to support and aid the Spanish nation, by clearing Portugal so immediately of the French that the British Army could instantly commence preparations for moving into Spain. But Sir Hugh Dalrymple's plain honest memoir of the whole transaction and Colonel Napier's history of the war in Spain so completely refute all the nonsense that was talked and written about that convention, that there is no necessity to dwell any longer upon it. Anyone who reads those works will see upon what sandy foundation all the senseless outcry was made; but it served the ministers' object, and, whenever any political object is to be gained, the unfortunate military commander will always be sacrificed, *right or wrong!* It has, I am sorry to say, been the case throughout the history of England ever since William III., and, I fear, will continue so.

Very soon after this convention was put into execution Sir Hugh Dalrymple was recalled, and went to England to account for his conduct before a court of inquiry; and, as Sir Arthur Wellesley was as much implicated in the business, he was sent for too; so that the army was deprived of his valuable services for a long time. Sir John Moore was appointed by the king's positive command to be commander-in-chief of the army ordered to enter Spain, notwithstanding the ministry were hostile to him; and I believe, from letters I saw, and from what Sir John Moore told me himself, that Lord Castlereagh and Mr. Canning did all they could to prevent his appointment, but that old George III. was immovable upon that point, and said, 'No other man but Moore should have the command of that army.'

And well did he justify the king's confidence in him, and sacredly did he keep the safety and honour of that army and the trust reposed in him to the last hour of his existence, when he sealed it with his blood! Upon Sir John Moore's appointment he made me his *aide-de-camp*, which was the highest honour I could receive at that time, and proved that I had, by constant zeal and attention to my duty, gained his approbation. Otherwise he never would have appointed me, being one of those characters who allowed no personal feelings to interfere with what he thought just; and, although very fond of me, and always treating me like a son, yet, had there been any other captain in the regiment who he conceived deserved it more, he would have appointed him his *aide-de-camp*, although personally he liked me better. Indeed, he told me this on two different occasions before, when I had hoped to be his *aide-de-camp*, and when he made others to whom he had no particular attachment.

Before giving up the command of my company and joining the general, I went with a detachment of my regiment under the command of Major Arbuthnott to escort the French garrison of Elvas to Lisbon, where they were to embark and be conveyed to France. We had a very agreeable march, but part of the French troops, a Swiss regiment (whose colonel the Portuguese had attempted to assassinate), behaved very mutinously and riotously, and attempted to plunder the inhabitants; so we were obliged to threaten them with punishment. I saw a French soldier behave ill, and on speaking to the commander of the troops he went up to the man, who was rather mutinous and insolent, upon which the colonel instantly pulled out his pistol, presented it at the soldier's head and snapped it at him; luckily it did not go off, or he would have shot him dead. This could not be done in our army, as no officer can either shoot or flog a British soldier upon his own authority. Nothing can be worse than permitting those in authority to have absolute power over their fellow-creatures, for the chances are they would make a bad use of it. In fact no man should be entrusted with absolute power; human nature is not proof against the sweets of power; it must be curbed.

Upon our arrival at Lisbon with the French garrison, I joined Sir John Moore and commenced my duty as *aide-de-camp*. One day I was going to purchase a sabre, when Sir John Moore told me not to do so, but to buy a straight sword, sharp on both edges. The reason he gave was this: when a colonel, he commanded a storming party at the fort of Calvi, in Corsica, and just as he mounted the top of the breach and was forcing his way in, a French grenadier, one of those defending the entrance, was on the point of plunging his bayonet into him, when Moore, seeing his only chance of life was to run his sword through the man, did so and killed him on the spot; now if he had not had a *straight* sword, but a sabre, he would not have been able to run the grenadier through the body, and would have been killed himself. So I did as he desired me, and purchased a straight one; but, thank God, I was lucky enough never to use my sword in the same way as Sir John Moore was forced to use his (and he told me he never should forget the horrid sensation it gave him when drawing the sword out of the man's body, and that it was always a painful recollection to him), although I did command a storming party, as you shall hear in due time.

After a great deal of bother and much labour on the part of Sir John Moore, and indeed every branch of the service, the army was put in motion, and began its long and toilsome march for Spain in high order and higher spirits, and a more glorious set of fellows never was seen. But we wanted a great requisite in the art of war, and that was *experience*, for, except some few generals and superior officers, we had none of us seen war on a large scale; indeed the greatest part never had seen a regular campaign except that of Vimiera a few months before. Our staff was inexperienced, our commissariat perfectly ignorant of their business, as well as our paymaster's department.

In short, as this was the first British Army (since the expedition to Egypt in 1801) which was assembled to act on the continent against the ablest and most experienced troops in Europe, no wonder we were often embarrassed and not in as good order (afterwards) as we should have been had we been old soldiers *au fait* at our business. However, after various difficulties, marches, fatigues, and disappointments to the general as well as his army, we all joined at Salamanca, one of the finest cities in Spain, and famous for its learned university, where the greater part of the Spanish nobility and priesthood are educated, as well as a large proportion of Irish, for the priesthood of that country. While we were there, the principal of the college was Dr. Curtis, an Irishman, and now (1828) the Catholic Primate of Ireland. He was a great favourite of Sir John Moore and afterwards of the Duke of Wellington, and I believe both those generals found him of great use to them, and could always rely upon his word and conduct.

After various difficulties, political as well as military, Sir John Moore made a forward movement towards the enemy, in order to form a junction with Sir David Baird's corps, lately arrived from England and landed at Coruña, in the north of Spain, where, from the great apathy of the Spaniards, who would not give the smallest aid to Baird, and the general inexperience of his army, and particularly his commissariat and paymaster-general's departments, he was unable to move and join Sir John Moore. Sir David had twice made the attempt, and latterly had got as far as Benevento, but from false information respecting both the strength and position of the enemy's army, as well as ignorance of Sir John Moore's movements, by which, of course, he would be guided, he was again obliged to retrograde, and was in full march for Coruña when a despatch from Sir John Moore informed him that he was on his march towards Sahagun, where he expected Sir David would join him, and then he would make a forced march and attack Soult at Saldanha.

During our march to Sahagun, our cavalry under Lord Paget (afterwards Marquis of Anglesea) and Sir Charles Stewart (afterwards Marquis of Londonderry) had two or three smart affairs with the French cavalry, and were always successful. The very morning of our arrival at Sahagun Lord Paget had given them a dressing, making several prisoners, besides a number being killed and wounded. I found a number of the prisoners confined in a large cellar, where they were badly off, many wounded, and nothing to eat or drink. Of course I immediately mentioned this to the general, and he desired me to order the commissary to provide them with wine and bread.

This being done, the poor fellows were as merry as possible, and began dancing and singing; and one of them, to my great amusement, took a little fiddle from his pocket and commenced playing quadrilles with as much energy and life as though he was playing to a parcel of ladies in a ball-room. The next night we were joined by Sir David Baird's corps, and the head of the column was in motion to move on Marshal Soult's corps of the French army, which we were to attack at daylight on the following morning, when just as Sir John Moore was mounting his horse, and I was actually giving him his pistols, a Spanish peasant came up, and asking for the general-in-chief, put a note into his hand from the Marquis de Romana, the Spanish general, which gave information that Napoleon had changed his plan of operations in consequence of Sir John Moore's movement in advance, and was inarching with great speed down on the British Army with an immense force.

The instant Sir John Moore had read this letter he saw there was no time to be lost, as Napoleon would be on his rear and cut off his retreat through Galicia, and that a battle and victory over Soult could be of no advantage, but most probably be the cause of the total destruction of the army by the immense numbers of the enemy in front and rear who were pouring down on our small force from all directions. He immediately ordered the troops to counter-march, and we commenced our memorable retreat to Coruña, in the north of Spain, and the nearest point towards England, to which port the transports were afterwards ordered, to be ready to embark the army, as the general foresaw that it would be impossible to remain in Spain, and that the great effort would be to arrive at the place of embarkation *without a battle* if possible, and then sail with the army to some other place in the Peninsula, where we could be of more use.

The soldiers, who do not ever like a *retreat*, as they are obliged to make forced marches and undergo much fatigue, and suffer many hardships and privations, very soon got into a state of disorder, plundering the inhabitants, breaking open the wine vaults, getting beastly drunk, and straggling over the country, by which means great numbers were made prisoners by the enemy, and many killed by the justly enraged Spaniards.

At Benevento, a large town where we halted for one night, one of Napoleon's generals, and a relation of his own, called Lefevre Desnouettes, commanding a division of cavalry of the Imperial Guard, crossed the river and formed up his troops on a plain, upon which our Hussars under Sir Charles Stewart attacked them with great spirit, and in a very short time completely upset them, killing, wounding, and taking many prisoners, among whom was the general himself, who, being attacked by a couple of our hussars as he made an attempt to gain a ford, and being slightly wounded in the head, surrendered himself just as Sir Charles Stewart came up, who sent him to headquarters, where he arrived magnificently dressed in scarlet and gold as general of the Imperial Hussars.

Sir John Moore received him in the kindest manner, and seeing he was bleeding, immediately sent for some water and washed the wound himself, gave him fresh linen, &c., and sent in a flag of truce to request that his baggage might be allowed to come to him, which was permitted by Napoleon, and that night it arrived, with several horses and servants, &c., for the French generals have always a great proportion of baggage. When General Lefevre was dressed, and just before we sat down to dinner, Sir John Moore asked him if there was anything he wished, upon which Lefevre cast a glance at his side (his sword having been taken from him when made prisoner) and then looked at Sir John Moore, who, comprehending what he meant, with all the high feeling of a soldier and the grace of a perfect gentleman, unbuckled his own sword from his side and presented it to his prisoner, who, I grieve to say for the honour of his profession, deserved it not.

Lefevre Desnouettes *broke* his *parole of honour*, and made his escape from England some time after Moore's death! was justly disgraced by Napoleon, though he was allowed to serve afterwards, and at last died an exile in America. What has become of the sword I know not, but I can never forget how much we were all struck with Sir John Moore's conduct; the whole transaction was perfect, the kindness of expression and the soldier-like sympathy which was apparent in the British general's countenance was perfectly beautiful; but was there ever an act of his during his life that was not perfect?

If ever any of you, my boys, should, by the fortune of war, be made prisoner, and be on your parole, and should so horribly disgrace yourself by breaking that parole, I would never see you again; indeed, I should use every endeavour to have you sent back to the nation whose army made you a prisoner. A man's word once given is *sacred*, and nothing should induce him to break it. If he does, his honour is gone, and he forfeits all claim to the character of a gentleman, and should never be treated as one.

We proceeded on our retreat towards Coruña. Our march was made with great rapidity, and the men and officers were obliged to be eternally under arms, as the enemy pursued us as quickly as possible, in hopes of bringing us to action while in a more open country than he knew we should be in once we reached Astorga. This often obliged the rearguard under General Paget to be many hours without food or rest, as they had not time to cook. There never was any want of provisions, but great want of time to cook them, and this it was impossible to prevent, as the enemy gave us no respite till we got to Astorga, where, notwithstanding that Sir John Moore had requested the Spanish general Romana not to quarter his army, but to leave that city and the road through Galicia free for the march of the British, we found the town crammed full of Spanish troops, and of course the arrival of our army made the confusion beyond anything. And here the army was in a highly disorganised state, breaking open stores, plundering the houses, &c., and a horrid scene of drunkenness in all the corps except General Paget's and the Guards at Villafranca. The general found it necessary to make an example by shooting a private of the 15th Hussars, whom Captain Pasley and myself caught plundering a house; and upon our laying hold of him he was most insolent, and struck Pasley. The facts being stated to the general, he was shot that morning; and this had some effect, but not much, I am sorry to say.

At Lugo, the French having only pursued us from Astorga with Marshal Soult's corps (as Buonaparte, who had passed in review at Astorga, two days after we left it, *ninety thousand* troops, had been obliged to hurry off with the Imperial Guards and other corps towards Germany, in consequence of Austria having declared war against him), we made a halt in order to rest the troops and if possible to give battle and cripple Soult's corps, which would enable us to retreat more leisurely and consequently more regularly. Sir John Moore took up an excellent position, and offered battle to the marshal, who, after a slight demonstration and a smart skirmish, in which we lost a few killed and wounded, thought it the most prudent thing to leave us quiet, as he felt sure we must move off the next day, and that he could not fail to have us at Coruña.

As I was riding along the position in the morning with some orders in a great hurry, and as I passed that part of the line where your Uncle Charles, who commanded the 50th Regiment, and his friend Major Stanhope were eating a famous dish of 'Irish stew' for breakfast, these two fellows, knowing that I dared not stop, ran up and put this savoury dish to my nose by way of tantalising me, who had been on horseback nearly all night and had not eaten anything for many hours, and then shouted out, 'You dainty dog, you can't eat Irish stew!' This will show you what merry fellows soldiers are, for we were then every moment expecting to be attacked by the enemy, and knew not if any one of us three should ever eat any dish again. There is an old song and a very true one which begins, '*How merrily we live that soldiers be!*' and it is one you should always put in practice whenever you can. Nothing like good and joyous spirits in a soldier. They will carry you a long day's march, for he that is gay and lively never flags.

At night the army was ordered to be put, as silently as possible, in movement, and we recommenced our rapid retreat, leaving the picquets to keep up the fires all through the night in order to deceive the enemy and gain several hours' march upon him, which we accordingly did, and the picquets joined us by a forced march before we halted for the night. The men, however, being very much disappointed at not having a battle, and being fatigued with the length and rapidity of the retreat which was absolutely necessary to save the army from destruction, became totally disorganised, and disregarding all discipline and throwing off the authority of their officers, detached themselves in large parties, straggling, drinking, and pillaging in the most shameful and infamous manner.

I saw several fellows quit their ranks and go off across the fields to plunder, and on riding up to one of them and ordering him to return instantly to his regiment, he swore he would not be ordered by me, and presented his rifle at my head; but luckily for me it missed fire, or I should have finished my career on the spot. I ought to have shot him with my pistol on the instant, or to have brought him a prisoner to the commander-in-chief, who would have ordered him to be shot, but I felt a dislike to have a fellow-creature put to death on my account. Now this was very wrong, as I should never have permitted my personal feelings to interfere with my duty to the service; and most probably, had I got that fellow shot, as he richly deserved, it would have been a great means of restoring discipline to the army, and might have frightened many soldiers from committing such crimes, and saved many a man's life being taken by the enraged peasants, or being cut down or made prisoners by the enemy's cavalry.

On that very day Sir John Moore halted the whole army and addressed each division upon its infamous, disgraceful conduct; he called upon the soldiers to recollect they were Englishmen, and not to disgrace their country and the bright lustre of the name of Britons by such disorders and such beastly drunkenness! He told them that rather than command men who behaved in such an infamous manner, he prayed to God that the first bullet fired by the enemy might enter his heart, for he would much rather be dead than command such an army! This seemed to produce some effect, and I do think their conduct improved after that day.

But the men were not so much to blame as the officers; for I fearlessly assert that, generally speaking, the officers of that army were more engaged in looking after themselves and their own comforts, and openly murmuring against the commander-in-chief, than in looking after the soldiers and keeping up proper discipline. I know that there were many exceptions to this censure—notably Sir John Hope, Lord William Bentinck, and Sir Rowland Hill, who exerted themselves in every way to keep up the discipline; and the *reserve* under General Paget, which, as forming the rearguard, had double the work and fatigue of any other division; for every officer and man, from the general who gave the example to the youngest soldier in the regiments, did their duty with spirit and with zeal—I, from being on the staff, had many opportunities of observing the conduct of the various divisions of that army, and the more I reflect upon what I witnessed, the more convinced I am that the great cause of the disorganised state of the troops was mainly owing to the supineness of the general officers (excepting those named above) and to the imprudent language they used themselves, and permitted their staff to make use of, when speaking of the retreat and the conduct of it by the commander-in-chief.

I shall take this opportunity of impressing upon your minds that no officer or soldier while upon service has a right to publicly (and it is much better let alone privately) canvass or blame the conduct of the general who commands that army for the movements, whether in advance or retreat, which he thinks it advisable to order. Officers *are to obey* and exercise their respective duties without a murmur, and with zeal and cheerfulness; and if they are under deprivations and enduring hardships and great fatigue, whatever their opinion (and every man has a right to his opinion) may be of the necessity of such things, they must learn to keep it to themselves. It is impossible for the officers of an army to know the commander-in-chief's reasons for making movements either retrograde or in advance; and what to the army may appear hard, unjust, foolish, or rash, may be the very thing by which the commander-in-chief, from his knowledge of circumstances and information, is enabled to preserve his army from being crippled or destroyed by an overwhelming force, or by which he deceives the enemy and defeats his projects.

In short, as long as a general is entrusted with the command of an army by his king, he and he alone is the proper judge of the movements of that army, and is responsible to his country for its safety and conduct; and the man who seconds his general, according to his rank and situation, with zeal, ability, and cheerfulness without regard to his own opinion (whatever that opinion may be) will best deserve the thanks of his country and be the truest soldier. If ever it should fall to my lot to command a body of troops, should I find any individual of it presuming to canvass my conduct, or murmuring at any duty, however severe and harassing, which may fall to his share, I would instantly send him off; he should not remain one day with the army, no matter what his rank might be![1] so mind, young gentlemen, and never either canvass the conduct of your commander, or murmur at what you are ordered to perform, and particularly on no account whatever let the soldiers see a *shade of discontent* on your countenances; if you do, you will be totally unfit, in my opinion, to be in the army, and the sooner you quit it the better.

During the retreat I was one night sent by Sir John Moore with despatches of great importance to Sir David Baird, which were to be forwarded by him to General Fraser, who commanded a division which was to march by another route, and this despatch was to countermand the former order and desire him to resume his place in the column. This despatch was delivered by me, after riding all night in a heavy storm of rain, sleet, and snow, at four or five o'clock in the morning, Sir John Moore having told me that if I did not ride fast I should be too late to catch Sir David before he had marched, as his division would be under arms before daylight and moving off the ground.

---

1. 'Our own Correspondent' would have had a rough time of it under Sir George Napier, or Sir Charles either!—Ed. (W.N.)

However, as I said, I arrived just after day had broke, about five o'clock, and going direct to Sir David's quarters I found him and his *aide-de-camp*, Captain Alexander Gordon, in bed in the same room, and not thinking of moving. Sir David, having read the despatch, asked me if I was to carry the one enclosed to General Eraser, or was he, Sir David, to forward it. I replied I received no orders to do more than deliver my despatch as speedily as possible to him, but that if he had no officer to send, and would give me a fresh horse (my own and the dragoon's who accompanied me being completely knocked up), I was perfectly ready to go on. He said, 'Oh, no, if you were not ordered to go I shall send it on by an orderly dragoon.' I then repeated I was not ordered, but was perfectly ready to do so if he had not an officer to send, as I knew it was of consequence.

Sir David replied in a very gruff manner, 'Sir, that's my business; I shall send it by a dragoon.' Of course I was silent, and then, asking him if he had any commands, I took my departure (after resting my horse) on my way back to meet the general, and in a few hours I was overtaken by an officer who told me that the orderly dragoon sent by Sir David had got drunk and lost the despatch, so that by the time Sir John Moore was informed of this and a fresh despatch written and sent off, many hours were lost and the division of General Fraser quite knocked up with the length of march it was forced to make in order to regain the main body. Sir John Moore was deeply vexed at this, but as the thing was done and could not be undone he said very little about it to Sir David.

Not so Colonel Graham (now Lord Lynedoch), who was very angry indeed, and made no scruple of loudly expressing it both before Sir John Moore and to Sir David Baird. At length we arrived at Coruña after a most arduous and harassing retreat, the rearguard under General Paget being almost constantly in action with the enemy's advance. Upon arriving at Coruña there were no transports, as the wind and stormy weather had delayed them in Vigo Bay, where it had been Sir John Moore's first intention to have retreated and embarked the army; indeed, one division of the troops under General Robert Craufurd did go by that route and embarked there. The transports not having arrived was very unfortunate, as, had they been all ready, as Sir John Moore fully expected, the whole army would have been embarked without fighting that battle which, although so glorious for the honour of the army, was the cause of England losing Sir John Moore, the best general she had except the Duke of Wellington, who at that time had not the experience and reputation of Sir John Moore.

The first thing Sir John Moore did was to take up as good a position as the strength of the army and other circumstances would permit; for, although there was a much stronger position, it did not offer the same advantages, for it was necessary to consider that as the object was to embark the army with as little loss as possible, the nearer our troops were to the place of embarkation the better, as, if we were forced to fight, let the result of the battle be what it might, embark we must, and, of course, the easiest manner of effecting that was Sir John Moore's main object; and the sequel proved him right in his judgement.

As soon as the troops were in position, they commenced preparing for embarking the stores and heavy artillery which were unnecessary in the camp. Then the order was given for shooting the dragoon horses, as there were no horse-ships to embark them in; besides, had there been ships, there was no time, and the poor animals were all half-dead already from fatigue and want of food, and were all foundered and suffering great pain. Now, if they had fallen into the hands of the enemy or of the Spaniards, the unfortunate brutes would have been worked to death, so it was better that they should be at once shot than left to live a few weeks longer in pain and misery. I mention this because there was a senseless outcry raised against the general for shooting the cavalry horses, which was absolutely necessary, and the only thing to be done in a military or humane point of view.

The troops received fresh ammunition, as what they had was wet and bad; also the unserviceable muskets were exchanged for new ones found in the Spanish stores, and which had been sent from England long before for the use of the Spaniards, who, instead of distributing them to the peasantry or to their troops, coolly locked them up in store! There were two powder magazines at some distance from the position of the army. These Sir John Moore very properly ordered to be blown up, as they would otherwise have fallen into the hands of the French. I never saw a more beautiful sight; but, I am sorry to say, a fine fellow, an officer of engineers who had the execution of this, was unfortunately blown up by going too near the place to see that the train was properly laid, and he had not time to escape before the whole blew up, and, of course, he was destroyed, poor fellow!

The same evening the transports arrived under convoy of several men-of-war, and immediately everything was embarked, such as the sick and wounded, the stores, heavy artillery, baggage, and staff horses that is, every staff-officer was allowed to embark one horse if he had one that was sound and worth embarking. That morning, before the ships arrived, as I was attending Sir John Moore riding to the position, he said to me: 'I have often been thought an unlucky man by my friends in consequence of being generally wounded in action, and some other events of my life, but I never thought so myself till now; and if the transports do not arrive this day, I shall certainly be convinced I am an unlucky fellow, and that fate has so decreed'

BATTLE OF CORUÑA

On the morning of the battle—*viz.*, January 16, 1809, I had just returned from delivering some orders in the camp, when the commander-in-chief desired me to order the horses and accompany him to the position. We had just mounted when we heard a shot from a gun, and we instantly galloped off, and arrived as the troops were all under arms and the whole line preparing to sustain the attack of the enemy, who was advancing in strong columns down upon us under cover of a heavy fire from their batteries which commanded our position, and a cloud of sharpshooters in their front. The fire from the artillery was destructive, and killed many of our brave fellows; but nothing could shake the steadiness or disturb the order of our troops; and, as the enemy closed upon our line, the general gave the order to advance, and placed himself in front of the 42nd Highlanders, to whom he was addressing himself and telling them not to forget what he had seen them so often do under his command in Holland and Egypt.

He had just ordered me to go and bring up the Guards to the support of Lord William Bentinck's brigade (consisting of the 4th, 42nd, and 50th Regiments), where he was himself, and which was most furiously attacked by the enemy. I had just put spurs to my horse, when, turning my head to look at what was going on, I saw Sir John Moore's horse give a spring into the air, and the next moment the general fell to the ground, and was instantly caught up and supported by Captain Hardinge (now Major-General Sir Henry Hardinge,[2] and one of the first men in the British Army in every respect).

The whole passed like a vision before my eyes, but I saw enough to know that the general was wounded. My first impulse was to return to him, but, in an instant I recollected that he had sent me with most

---

2. Major-General Sir Henry Hardinge, G.C.B., was born in 1785, became Governor-General of India in 1844, was created Viscount Hardinge of Lahore in 1846, commander-in-chief of the British Army in 1852, field-marshal in 1855, and died in 1856.

important and urgent orders for the Guards, and, bitter and painful as were the feelings which agitated me at that instant, my duty told me to proceed, though my affections strongly urged me to go back. The struggle was momentary; duty triumphed, and in a few minutes I was delivering my orders to the commanding officer of the Guards, and never was I gratified by again seeing my beloved general and friend alive.

On my return, I heard how dreadfully and mortally he was wounded, and that he was carried to the rear. Sir David Baird, than whom a more gallant soldier never breathed, had been severely wounded early in the action, and was taken on board ship, where his arm was obliged to be removed at the shoulder-joint, and consequently the command devolved on Sir John Hope, one of the most able officers in the British Army, as well as the most noble-minded of men.

As it would have been very improper to have left the field, and being aware that Colonel Anderson, Sir John's oldest and dearest friend, was with him. I attached myself to General Hope, who was now, in fact, commander-in-chief. During the battle I had seen your uncle Charles charging the enemy at the head of his regiment, the 50th, with his friend and second in command, Major Stanhope. They had taken the village of Elvina, and were driven out again three times, for the enemy, being able to reinforce their attacking troops after every repulse, at last overpowered the 50th, which was forced to retreat. At this period Captain Stanhope, a brother of the major, and myself were riding towards the 50th in order to make some inquiries respecting our brothers, and I was just at the rear of the regiment, when I met some soldiers carrying the body of an officer who was shot through the heart.

I jumped from my horse, removed with trembling hands the handkerchief which was over the face, and beheld the pale and ghastly countenance of my valued friend, Charles Stanhope! I had no time to shed a tear to his memory—his poor brother was approaching; I quickly remounted my horse, and, meeting him, said, 'Come along, we must instantly return to General Hope;' at the same time I seized the bridle of his horse, and turned him round before he had time to recognise the bleeding corpse of his gallant brother. As we went along I told him what had happened, and he bore it as every soldier ought, but could not resist the desire of going to take a last look at poor Charles. To this I could not object, but did not accompany him.

While riding about with General Hope, we came to a narrow

place where we could only pass singly, and as the enemy had a vast number of sharpshooters, they fired at every officer as he passed. Captain Woodford, who went before me, got severely wounded in the foot; I crossed without being touched; but the poor fellow who followed me, young Burrard, got shot in the chest, and died two days afterwards on board ship.

We rode about the field of battle, first to one brigade, then another, General Hope directing and encouraging the troops in every part. At last, coming to where the 50th was hotly engaged, Captain Clunes, the eldest captain of the regiment, came up to us, and, addressing General Hope, said: 'Sir, our commanding officer, Major Napier, is killed; we have no field officer left; our ammunition is expended; what are we to do?' You cannot, my children, conceive the bitterness of my feelings at that moment. I had a few hours before seen the general I revered as a father carried off the field mortally wounded; I had met the bleeding, lifeless body of my friend, Charles Stanhope; and now I learned that the brother I loved, who was my friend, my adviser, my constant companion, was among the slain, and that it was denied to me to close his dying eyes! And then the thought of my poor mother's misery! May the anguish I then suffered never be your lot.

Towards evening, the enemy having been repulsed in all their attacks, and driven by our troops with great slaughter far beyond our original position, the battle ceased. Then, the evening being far advanced, Sir John Hope returned to the town to give orders and superintend the embarkation of the army during the night, as it was not judged advisable to delay it, the French being still very much superior to us both in men and guns. I did not return to the town with the general, as I heard from some of the officers of the regiment that they thought my brother was only wounded, and that he must be lying somewhere on the field of battle. It being now dark, I went over the ground with a torch in my hand, and looked at the body of every officer I could find, in the melancholy but vain hope of once more seeing the countenance, though in death, of my beloved brother Charles, and that I might satisfy my mind that he was dead.

At last, finding it hopeless to search any longer, and in the bitterness of my sorrow, it came across me that perhaps he had been taken to the hospital in town. As quick as the thought seized me, I went off to the house appointed for receiving the wounded, and, on arriving, commenced afresh my melancholy search. Not a wounded man in the hospital escaped my glance—but in vain! No dear brother was to be found, and no one could give me any other tidings but that they saw him killed.

With a heavy heart I turned my sorrowful steps to the headquarter house. On entering I saw no light; I heard no sound, no movement— all was silent as the grave. A cold dread chill struck upon my heart as I ascended the gloomy stairs and opened the opposite door from whence I imagined I heard the half-stifled sob of grief. Oh, God! what was my horror, my misery, my agony! Sir John Moore lay stretched on a mattress; a dreadful wound bared the cavity of his chest; he had just breathed his last. The lofty spirit which so lately animated that beautiful, though now cold and bleeding, form had taken its flight to the regions of the great and good, there to receive the reward of all the sufferings, toils, and ingratitude it had experienced in this world of sorrow and disappointment. Yes; noble spirit of Moore, thou wilt be recorded by history as a bright example for ages to come of all the attributes which adorn the soldier, all the virtues which dignify the man!

Never shall I forget the scene that room displayed on that fatal night. Colonel Anderson, who had been from youth the tried friend and companion of his general, was kneeling, with his arm supporting Sir John Moore's head, with blanched cheeks, half-parted colourless lips, and his eyes intently fixed on that face whose smile of approbation and affection had been his pride and delight for years; but the look of keen anguish that Anderson's countenance expressed is far beyond my powers of description. Next in this group stood Colborne, whose firm and manly countenance was relaxed and overcast with thoughtful grief, as though he pondered more on his country's than on private sorrow, for he felt and deeply mourned the amount of England's loss. Then high-spirited, guileless Harry Percy, pouring forth in convulsive sobs the overflowing of his warm and generous heart; and poor James Stanhope completely struck down and overwhelmed by the double loss of his brother and his friend.

As though lost in this imperfect sketch, not least absorbed in the deep anguish of despair, stood his faithful and devoted servant 'François,' bending over his master's mangled body, his hands clasped in speechless agony, his face as pale as the calm countenance he wildly gazed upon. That eye which was wont to penetrate the inmost soul was glazed in death. That manly, graceful form, the admiration of the army, lay stretched a bloody, lifeless corpse; the great spirit had quitted its earthly habitation; all around was sad and gloomy. Moore was dead!

Such was the scene which presented itself to my view on entering that sorrowful chamber of death. And although now twenty years have passed, the whole is perfectly fresh in my memory, and I do not think I have forgotten one of the melancholy and heart-rending circumstances that accompanied Sir John Moore's death. His funeral was, as he always had desired it might be, that of a soldier, and is most feelingly and correctly described in those beautiful verses of Mr. Wolfe, '*Not a drum was heard, not a funeral note*,' &c.[3] Your uncle William's pen is the only one that has ever done justice to his character and conduct as a man and a general. Read it often; the language is beautiful, chaste, and eloquent, for it is the language of the heart. The history of the Coruña campaign is one of the best studies for a military man. In Sir John Moore's character we have a model for everything that marks the obedient soldier, the persevering, firm, and skilful general; the inflexible and real patriot who sacrificed all personal feeling to his country's weal; the truly virtuous and honourable man; the high-minded, finished, and accomplished gentleman.

Early on the morrow of that sad and dreary night Colonel Colborne and myself went on board the *Audacious*, 74 gun ship, Captain Gosling, having with much difficulty reached her, as in consequence of the enemy bringing some guns to the heights which in fact commanded the bay, and opening a fire on the transports, they were cutting away their cables and were in much confusion, and it was a service of danger to get through them.

I shall here state what your Uncle Charles related to me after he returned to England. You know that, as it afterwards proved, he was only badly wounded, and having had his life saved by a French drummer, he was taken to a part of the enemy's position from whence he could perceive the British army, the town, and the fleet. During the night, as he lay on the ground, he heard from some of the French officers that the English commander-in-chief was killed. He had seen his friend Major Stanhope shot by his side, and he was ignorant of my fate, but lay expecting every moment that a flag of truce would be sent in, and that I should be the bearer of it to make inquiries about him and to exchange him for some French officer, as he knew not that he had been reported killed. (Had it been known he was a prisoner, the flag of truce would of course have gone in, and I with it.)

He says, when morning broke, and he saw all the fleet in the bay beneath, his spirits cheered up, feeling confident that ere long the

---

3. See Appendix 1.

wished-for flag of truce would make its appearance; but when he perceived the ships sailing away one after another, and at last the only remaining one in full sail, his heart died within him, and he kept straining his eyes looking after them till they were completely out of sight. He then felt in perfect solitude and misery; he was sure I must have been killed; and, with the many severe wounds he was suffering from himself, he felt as if he was dying without a human being who cared for him to close his eyes. I can easily conceive the mental pain he endured during these twenty-four hours. However, when he was taken into the town and lodged at the American Consul's house, where every care and kindness was shown to him by that gentleman, as well as by the French officers, particularly Marshals Soult and Ney, he soon resumed his wonted cheerfulness, and in the course of some weeks he recovered sufficiently to enjoy himself as well as a prisoner can.

The day we embarked Colonel Graham (Lord Lynedoch) told me it was the intention of General Hope to send me home with the despatch of the battle, as Colonel Graham knew that Sir John Moore had meant to send me if there was a battle. However, be this as it may, Sir David Baird settled all that by ordering General Hope to make his report of the action to him as commander-in-chief, and saying that he, Sir David, should send his own nephew and *aide-de-camp* Captain Gordon home with the despatch, which he accordingly did, notwithstanding the remonstrances of General Hope, Colonels Graham and Murray. So indelicate a thing was never done before under similar circumstances. Sir David had been wounded by almost the first shot fired, and had left the field with his staff; and after the battle was over, and upon General Hope sending to him for orders respecting the embarkation, his answer was, 'General Hope commands, he must act and take all responsibility on himself; I shall not interfere;' yet the moment all was effected, *viz.*, the battle gained, the whole army embarked, and the fleet under sail, and no further responsibility, he retook the command in order to send his own nephew home with the despatch.

I must do justice to my friend Captain Gordon, by saying that he himself remonstrated with his uncle, Sir David, upon the impropriety of sending him instead of Sir John Moore's staff, but the only reply he got was, 'If you don't wish to go, I shall send Captain Baird.' Of course, after that, Gordon went. He told me this himself just before he started, and repeated it to me when I met him in London afterwards.

Sir John Hope went upon his arrival in England to Sir David Dundas, who was then commander-in-chief (the Duke of York having resigned in consequence of a rascally conspiracy against him, carried on from motives of private malice and revenge by that despicable character, Colonel Wardle, and supported by the Opposition of the day in the House of Commons from mere party motives, as I verily believe not one of them had either the good of the country or the honour and interest of the army at heart; and the proof was that before two years the whole country loudly called for His Royal Highness to be replaced at the head of that army to whose honour and interest he had devoted all his thoughts and actions, and which, by his assiduity and zeal, he had brought to the highest state of discipline and happiness; for under his rule every man got justice, and all were treated with kindness.

It was far otherwise before His Royal Highness was its chief; and very different were the feelings of officers and men under Sir David Dundas, who, although a very clever and able man, was ill-tempered, morose, and often very unjust; and long and loud was the shout of joy when the Duke of York took the command of the British Army). As I said above, Sir John Hope went to Sir David Dundas and spoke to him respecting me. Sir David said it was not his fault, he could not help it, and that I was a young man, and he did not see that I had anything to complain of. So having failed in that attempt to get what was only justice, I tried another way. At this time it was determined to send General Beresford to Portugal, to take command of the Portuguese army and put it into some kind of order, for which purpose twelve or fourteen captains of the British Army were to get the rank of major in their own service, and that of lieutenant-colonel in the Portuguese Army and the command of battalions. I made application to Sir David Dundas for one of these commissions, but was refused, Sir David saying I was too young a captain (I having been then nearly six years in that rank).

Well, when the *Gazette* came out no less than *twelve* of the *fourteen* captains appointed were junior to me in rank. So much for Sir David's justice in giving as his reason for not promoting me that I was too young a captain. In the same manner, two years afterwards, upon being asked by the Duke of Richmond to promote me, I having been all the intervening time on service and wounded, he coolly replied I was a young officer and had no claims. That was the last application ever made on my part; and, thank God, in *one year* after I had the satisfaction of being a lieutenant-colonel in spite of old Dundas; and every rank unsolicited, but given to me by Lord Wellington for my conduct in the field, as his despatches will attest, as well as his private letters to my mother. My two brothers also received the same marks of his approbation of their conduct; and we all feel higher gratification in our present rank, gained on the field of battle, than had we been generals by any other interest.

Sir David Dundas also did great injustice to your Uncle Charles upon the occasion of Coruña; for, in consequence of his being made a prisoner, Sir David refused to give him the rank of lieutenant-colonel, which was given to every major in command of a regiment upon that memorable day. At first, as Charles was supposed to be killed, of course no one thought about the matter, but when it appeared he was not killed, and that he returned to England and was exchanged, then he demanded the same promotion as the other majors commanding regiments. But old Sir David, who had the greatest antipathy to giving any man promotion who was not as old as himself, refused upon the plea of his being taken prisoner. The fact was, the crusty old fellow could not bear the idea of promotion; and, except his money, he would sooner part with anything else. However, thank God, the old boy is gone, and the Lord defend us from ever seeing such another at the head of the army.[4]

The second day after we embarked, my poor friend and brother *aide-de-camp*, Captain Burrard. son of Sir Harry Burrard, died on board of the wound he had got in the chest. He was a fine young man, a great favourite with everybody, and, had he been permitted to live, I have no doubt would have distinguished himself as an officer. It was melancholy to see his body consigned to the deep. In the heat of battle the mind is so employed and excited that our friends drop around us without our having time to think of their loss; but, when all excitement is over, and the mind cool and relaxed, to see your wounded comrades end their sufferings on a deathbed; to observe the last convulsive pang of death; to see their remains wrapped in a shroud and then thrown overboard; to hear the splash of the deep waters; see the waves roll over the spot and leave no trace behind, leaves a deep gloom

---

4. Sir Charles Napier used to give an amusing account of his interview with Sir D. Dundas on this or some other occasion of his asking for promotion. The commander-in-chief received him very kindly, asked after his health, advised him to wear flannel, but not a word would he say about promotion. Whenever Sir Charles mentioned the subject, the old gentleman replied, 'Wear flannel, major, wear flannel;' and finally bowed him out of the room, exclaiming, 'Wear flannel, major, wear flannel.'—Ed. (W.N.)

upon the spirits not easily thrown off. Such was poor Burrard's funeral; such my feelings; and every man on board shed a tear—a manly tear—to the memory of the youthful and the brave!

I had nearly forgotten to tell you that your poor mother's brother, young William Craig (who had been quite knocked up, and was ill on board one of the ships), the moment he heard the first shot fired by the enemy, got out of his bed, dressed himself, and, landing, went off to his regiment, the 52nd, where he behaved so gallantly as to attract the notice of his commanding officer, Colonel Barclay, and also that of the general commanding the division, General Paget, both of whom praised him highly.

Upon my arrival in England I went up to London to my mother, and, after being at home a few days, I went to see Sir John Moore's mother, who was seventy-five years old when her son was killed. She was one of the finest old women imaginable, dotingly fond of her son, and proud of that high spotless character and military fame which had gained him the approbation and confidence of his king and country, and to which alone he owed the command of the British Army in the Peninsula, where he fell at the age of forty-eight, having worked and *bled* for every gradation of rank from captain to lieutenant-general. His high-minded mother tried to console herself for his loss by the knowledge that John (as she called him) had fallen gloriously, and had upheld the honour of the British arms. She said:

> I would much sooner see my son brought home a bloody corpse than hear of his consenting to anything that could tarnish the glory of the army, or put his country to the blush.'

This was said just before the news of the battle and of her son's death arrived, and in consequence of a report that Sir John Moore had not fought, but entered into a convention with the enemy to be permitted to embark the British Army unmolested, and return to England without a battle! This he had been urged to do by some of the generals in his army, but he treated such advice with the contempt it deserved. He fought; he was victorious; but he fell! and his memory was calumniated by a heartless, ungrateful set of intriguers and base hired scribblers and libellers. It is humiliating to find such transcendent genius as Sir Walter Scott's lending itself to, and joining in, the shameful perversion of truth and the senseless eulogium of the conduct of the 'brave Spaniards,' the 'deserted Spaniards,' as if the Spaniards had fought and would have driven the French beyond the

Pyrenees, had they been supported by the British!

This was the language of all the government press, newspaper writers, pamphleteers, and poets, and followed up since by Mr. Southey, who, under the name of a *history* of the Spanish war, has sent forth to the public, as far as language goes, certainly a fine specimen of writing, but totally destitute of all pretension to truth; and, as a history of *war*, I defy any man to find a military idea in the whole work except where he gives an extract from a despatch. But, thank God, your uncle's history has done up the laureate's.

There is another anecdote of the lofty-minded mother of Sir John Moore which I must narrate, for it is worthy of the mother of such a son. The Government offered her a private pension of six or seven hundred a year, but she spurned the affront. 'No,' said the noble woman, 'I want no private bounty of the government as a recompense for the loss of my gallant, glorious son, and no pension will I take from ministers; but, if the Parliament of that country for which he so often bled and sacrificed his life thinks proper to mark its approbation of his conduct and services by a vote, however small the sum, to his aged mother, I will receive it with pride and gratitude as the gift of the nation in memory of its faithful and often tried servant, my lamented son.' But that Parliament, swayed by the party motives of the ministry, neglected his family, attempted to trample on his hallowed memory and wither the hard-earned laurels of a great and gallant soldier.

This was all owing to Mr. Canning, who was mean enough to attempt to cover his own and his colleagues' want of judgement, folly, presumption, and ignorance upon Spanish affairs by casting the blame upon him whose lamented, though glorious, death prevented their exposure to the public. I must also say that Lord Castlereagh did *not* join Mr. Canning, but gave just praise in his speech to the general's memory. I must also in justice say there were *some* who manfully raised their voices in his defence, and pointed him out to England as the saviour of her army from that destruction which would inevitably have been its fate, from the position it was placed in by the rash ignorance of our ministers, had Sir John's skill and firmness been one iota less prominent.

Among these upright, honest statesmen, none was more conspicuous than the 'soldier's friend,' his late Royal Highness the Duke of York (who had not at that moment resigned the command of the army); and the beautiful, just, and feeling tribute he paid to the character and memory of Sir John Moore in the following general order issued to the army must remain a lasting monument of His Royal Highness's impartial justice and generous feeling heart:—

General Order

The benefits derived to an army by the example of a distinguished commander do not terminate at his death; his virtues live in the recollection of his associates, and his fame remains the strongest incentive to great and glorious actions.

In this view the commander-in-chief, amidst the deep and universal regret which the death of Lieutenant-General Sir John Moore has occasioned, recalls to the troops the military career of that illustrious officer, for their instruction and imitation.

Sir John Moore from his youth embraced the profession with the feelings and sentiments of a soldier; he felt that a perfect knowledge and an exact performance of the humble but important duties of a subaltern officer are the best foundations for subsequent military fame; and his ardent mind, while it looked forward to those brilliant achievements for which it was formed, applied itself with energy and exemplary assiduity to the duties of that station.

In the school of regimental duty he obtained that correct knowledge of his profession so-essential to the proper direction of the gallant .spirit of the soldier; and he was enabled to establish a characteristic order and regularity of conduct because the troops found in their leader a striking example of the discipline which he enforced on others.

Having risen to command, he signalised his name in the West Indies, in Holland, and in Egypt.[5]

The unremitting attention with which he devoted himself to the duties of every branch of his profession obtained him the confidence of Sir Ralph Abercrombie; and he became the companion in arms of that illustrious officer, who fell at the head of his victorious troops in an action which maintained our national superiority over the arms of France.

Thus Sir John Moore at an early period obtained with general approbation that conspicuous station in which he gloriously terminated his useful and honourable life.

---

5. In Corsica, when a colonel, he stormed Fort Convention and the outworks of Calvi, which was followed by the conquest of the island. In Ireland he gained the Battle of Wexford, which was the prelude to the suppression of the Rebellion.

In a military character, obtained amidst the dangers of climate, the privations incident to service, and the sufferings of repeated wounds, it is difficult to select one point as a preferable subject for praise. It exhibits, however, one feature so particularly characteristic of the man and so important to the best interests of the service, that the commander-in-chief is pleased to mark it with his peculiar approbation.

The life of Sir John Moore was spent among the troops.

During the season of repose his time was devoted to the care and instruction of the officer and the soldier. In war he courted service in every quarter of the globe. Regardless of personal considerations he esteemed that to which his country called him the post of honour, and by his undaunted spirit and unconquerable perseverance he pointed the way to victory.

His country, the object of his latest solicitude, will rear a monument to his lamented memory; and the commander-in-chief feels that he is paying the best tribute to his fame by thus holding him forth as an example to the army.

By order of His Royal Highness the Commander-in-Chief.

    (Signed)   Harry Calvert,
                                        Adjutant-General.

Horse Guards, February 1, 1809.

My mother was never quite convinced that Charles was killed, because, as I could not find his body, she thought—rightly as it proved—that he was only wounded and must be a prisoner; and as about this time reports had reached us confirming her view in a slight degree, Lord Mulgrave, who was First Lord of the Admiralty, very kindly offered to send a sloop of war with a flag of truce to Coruña to make the necessary inquiries, and ascertain the truth of the report. When the ship arrived there, they found him recovering from the wounds he had received, which were four—a sabre cut across the top of his head; a bayonet plunged into his back as he lay on the ground; a shot in the leg; and grazed by a cannon ball which broke two of his ribs.

So, you see, he had a narrow escape. He would have been put to death had it not been for a French drummer, who saved his life by defending him from the fury of the soldiers. This drummer received from Napoleon the cross of the Legion of Honour for his conduct in having saved the life of a British officer. Marshal Soult, Duke of Dalmatia, was very kind to him; sent his own surgeon to dress his wounds; ordered him whatever money he wanted, and to be supplied from his own table with everything necessary to his comfort. When Marshal Soult left Coruña, Marshal Ney commanded, and from him he also received every kindness; and it was great grief to your uncle, as well as to all his family, when many years after, at the restoration of the Bourbons, and when Napoleon returned from Elba, to find Marshal Ney act so weakly in the first instance by his ridiculous speech to Louis XVIII., 'that he would bring back Napoleon a prisoner in an iron cage;' and, secondly, so wrongly in deserting Louis, breaking his oath to him, and going over to Napoleon at once.

Now, no man can feel greater gratitude to Marshal Ney for his treatment of your uncle, nor is there any person admires his transcendent military achievements more than myself, nor who more sincerely laments his melancholy fate, for he was most illegally put to death in violation of the Treaty of Paris; but that he acted most dishonourably and traitorously to Louis XVIII., who had placed full and entire confidence in him, I cannot conceive there is the least doubt; and, had he not come under the articles of the treaty at the surrender of Paris to the Duke of Wellington, I certainly think Louis would have been justified in putting him to death. I am very sorry the Duke of Wellington, even though he was so decidedly of opinion that Marshal Ney was excluded from the benefit of the treaty, did not demand his pardon from the King of France, who would not have dared to refuse him.[6]

You should learn from the conduct of the French to your uncle that to treat your enemy when in your power with every respect and kindness is the true characteristic of a brave man. None but the worthless coward insults or maltreats his prisoner; and, as the French officers are as brave as any men upon earth, so their conduct was humane and generous to one whom the for-tune of war had placed in their power. Marshal Ney, at the risk of Napoleon's displeasure, gave your uncle leave to go home on his parole not to serve against the French till he should be regularly exchanged, and as there were a few wounded soldiers and their wives and children who had been left behind, I believe about ten or fifteen individuals, Marshal Ney let them all return with him, and gave them a dollar each to find themselves with little

---

6. Since the above was in type it has been stated, on the authority of the late Duke of Wellington, that his father did his utmost privately to save the life of Marshal Ney, and that it was wholly in consequence of the absolute refusal of the King of France's ministers to advise him to grant the duke's request that he, as a matter of duty, abstained from publicly asking Louis XVIII. this favour.—Ed. (W.N.)

comforts on board for the voyage. Thus from first to last nothing could be better or more honourable than his and Marshal Soult's conduct to my brother. In a few days he arrived in England, and your grandmother received a scrap of paper upon which was written:

> *Hudibrass, you lie! you lie! for I have been in battle slain, and I live to fight again!*

Upon getting this note, which was written from Plymouth, your Aunts Louisa and Emily and myself set off to meet him, and, arriving at Exeter, who should we spy on top of the coach but your uncle in his old red coat, out at elbows, and covered with dust; his face pale, and his beard and whiskers as black as coal; in short, he looked like an old Chelsea pensioner. You will guess we made much of him, and returned to London immediately; and my dear mother was once more as happy as she deserved to be for the resignation and calm sorrow with which she submitted to God's will when she first heard of her son being killed, for no mother was more devotedly attached to her sons than she was. Thus you see that the mercy of God is unbounded, and that, if you bear all the dispensations of Providence with truly pious resignation and humble submission, you will not fail to reap the reward of your conduct either in this world or the next.

I have now finished the account of what I may call the first period of my military life, and I think I cannot close this part of my narrative better than by transcribing part of Sir John Hope's report of the battle of Coruña to Sir David Baird.

Extract

> Circumstances forbid us to indulge the hope that the victory with which it has pleased Providence to crown the efforts of the army can be attended with any very brilliant consequences to Great Britain. It is clouded by the loss of one of her best soldiers. It has been achieved at the termination of a long and harassing service. The superior numbers and advantageous position of the enemy, not less than the actual situation of this army, did not admit of any advantage being reaped from success. It must be, however, to you, to the army, and to our country, the sweetest reflection that the lustre of the British arms has been maintained amidst many disadvantageous circumstances.
>
> The army which had entered Spain amidst the finest prospects had no sooner completed its junction than, owing to the multi-

plied disasters that dispersed the native armies around us, it was left to its own resources. The advance of the British corps from the Duero afforded the best hope that the south of Spain might be relieved; but this generous effort to save the unfortunate people also afforded the enemy the opportunity of directing every effort of his numerous troops, and concentrating all his principal resources, for the destruction of the only regular force in the north of Spain.

You are well aware with what diligence this system has been pursued. These circumstances produced the necessity of rapid and harassing marches which had diminished the numbers, exhausted the strength, and impaired the equipment of the army. Notwithstanding all these disadvantages, and those more immediately attached to a defensive position, which the imperious necessity of covering the harbour of Coruña for a time had rendered it indispensable to assume, the native and undaunted valour of the British troops was never more conspicuous, and must have exceeded what even your own experience of that invaluable quality so inherent in them may have taught you to expect.

When everyone who had an opportunity seemed to vie in improving it, it is difficult for me, in making this report, to select particular instances for your approbation. The corps chiefly engaged were the brigades under Major-Generals Lord William Bentinck, and Manningham, and Leith, and the brigade of Guards under Major-General Warde. To these officers and the troops under their immediate orders the greatest praise is due. Major-General Hill and Colonel Catlin Crauford, with their brigades, on the left of the position, ably sup-ported their advanced posts.

The brunt of the action fell upon the 4th, 42nd, 50th, and 81st regiments, with parts of the brigade of Guards and the 26th Regiment. From Lieut.-Colonel Murray, quartermaster-general, and the officers of the general staff I received the most marked assistance. I had reason to regret that the illness of Brigadier-General Clinton, adjutant-general, deprived me of his aid. I was indebted to Brigadier-General Slade during the action for a zealous offer of his personal services, although the cavalry was embarked.

The greater part of the fleet having gone to sea yesterday evening, the whole being under weigh, and the corps in the embarkation necessarily much mixed on board, it is impossible at present to lay before you a return of our casualties. I hope the loss in numbers is not so considerable as might have been expected. If I was obliged to form an estimate I should say that I believe it did not exceed in killed and wounded from seven to eight hundred. That of the enemy must remain unknown, but many circumstances induce me to rate it at nearly double the above number.

We have some prisoners, but I have not been able to obtain an account of the number; it is not, however, considerable. Several officers of rank have fallen or been wounded, among whom I am at present enabled to state the names of Lieut.-Colonel Napier, 92nd Regiment, Majors Napier and Stanhope, 50th Regiment, killed. Lieut.-Colonel Winch, 4th Regiment, Lieut.-Colonel Maxwell, 26th Regiment, Lieut.-Colonel Fane, 59th Regiment, Lieut.-Colonel Griffiths, Guards, Majors Williams and Millar, 81st Regiment, wounded.

To you who are well acquainted with the excellent qualities of Lieut.-General Sir John Moore I need not expatiate on the loss the army and his country have sustained by his death. His fall has deprived me of a valuable friend, to whom long experience of his worth had sincerely attached me. But it is chiefly on public grounds that I must lament the blow. It will be the consolation of everyone who loved or respected his manly character, that after conducting the army through an arduous retreat with consummate firmness he has terminated a career of distinguished honour by a death that has given the enemy additional reason to respect the name of a British soldier.

Like the immortal Wolfe, he is snatched from his country at an early period of life spent in her service; like Wolfe, his last moments were gilded by the prospect of success, and cheered by the acclamation of victory; like Wolfe, also, his memory will forever remain sacred in that country which he sincerely loved. It remains for me only to express my hope that you will speedily be restored to the service of your country, and to lament the unfortunate circumstance that removed you from your station in the field and threw the momentary command into far less able hands.

            I have the honour to be, &c.
                (Signed)   John Hope,
                                        Lieutenant-General.

To Sir David Baird,
Lieut.-General Commanding the Army.

Chapter 3

The Peninsular War

I now commence the period when I again went on active service under one of the greatest captains that ever existed, whose splendid victories, unwearied perseverance, and firmness in carrying on the war which depended upon his skill and judgement, after seven years of continued hard service, and a series of bloody and glorious victories over the armies of France commanded by her best marshals, finally accomplished their total expulsion from the Peninsula, of which Napoleon had possessed himself in the most perfidious manner, and carried the glory of the British arms to the very walls of Toulouse, the capital of the south of France.

I must here mention that at this period General Graham (Lord Lynedoch), being employed on the staff in England, wrote to me, saying, that if I could be *aide-de-camp* to anyone after Sir John Moore, he trusted he need not say how happy he would be if I would take that situation on his personal staff. This was another proof of approbation and kindness from a man who has highly distinguished himself as a general by his military achievements and by the victory gained over the French Army at Barrosa, near Cadiz, one of the most splendid during the war. He was afterwards second in command to Lord Wellington, and then commander-in-chief of the army sent to Holland in 1813-14 to support the Dutch in their revolt from the sway of Napoleon; and at the peace of that year he was rewarded for his long and meritorious services by being created a Peer of the Realm. As my regiment was ordered to Portugal, of course I could not remain behind (although I had leave to do so on General Graham's staff), as that would have looked very like being afraid; besides, as I have already said, wherever an officer's regiment is ordered, it is his duty to go.

In giving you a narrative of my life during the campaigns I served under the Duke of Wellington, I shall not attempt any detailed account of the occurrences and battles that took place, as you will in time see them all minutely and beautifully described by your uncle as he proceeds in his history of the Peninsular War; but I will amuse you, as far as my memory serves me, with an account of the various anecdotes and circumstances to which I was either a witness or party concerned.

After a few months' stay in England my regiment, together with the 43rd and Rifle Corps, were ordered to embark at Deal under the command of Brigadier-General Robert Craufurd, in order to proceed to Portugal to reinforce Sir Arthur Wellesley, who had returned there, had taken the command of the British troops, and inarching immediately against Marshal Soult, who was with his corps at Oporto, crossed the river Douro in face of the enemy, attacked and completely overthrew him, killing, wounding, and making prisoners great numbers, and pursuing Soult so fast that he (Soult) was forced to abandon nearly all his artillery, baggage, ammunition, stores, &c.; in short, his army was totally dispersed, .and was obliged to make a run of it! Never was there a more decided victory or a more skilful military movement than Sir Arthur's passage of the Douro.

The Light Brigade, composed, as I have said, under Brigadier-General Craufurd, were upwards of three thousand men, and a magnificent troop of Horse Artillery under the command of Captain Ross (now Sir H. D. Ross[1]), and we embarked on board transports at Deal in May for Lisbon, where we arrived in about three weeks, having stopped at Portsmouth for some days on our passage down Channel. As soon as we had completed ourselves in baggage, mules, and various other equipments necessary for service, we proceeded to join the army which was marching on Talavera, in Spain, on the road to Madrid. Why we were sent to Lisbon I am at a loss to conceive, as the government at home was fully aware of the army being on the march to Spain long before we sailed, and had we landed at Oporto, we might have joined the Duke of Wellington at least ten days before we did, and have been in time for the Battle of Talavera, instead of too late by some hours. We had, however, a very agreeable march.

One day in the month of August, while marching under a burning sun, an officer of the 43rd told me my brother William was taken very ill, and was unable to proceed with the regiment. I immediately

---

1. Sir Hew Dalrymple Ross, K.C.B., was dangerously wounded at Badajos; he served in France and at Waterloo, and became adjutant-general of artillery.

went to him, and found he was very ill indeed, and in consequence of the quantity of blood the surgeon had found it necessary to take from him, he could not stand; so I got a bullock car, and placing him in it on some straw, I went to Placentia with him, to the hospital which had been established there. Upon arriving the commandant, gave me a good quarter for him, and the doctors having visited him and ordered medicine, &c., I put him into a comfortable warm bed, and in about five or six hours and a good sleep, he being out of all danger, I left him in the care of his servant and the doctor, and started to overtake the regiment, which was no easy matter, as an express had arrived with orders for the brigade to make.a forced march and join the army as quick as possible, as it was engaged with the enemy; so upon my arriving at the village where I expected to find my regiment bivouacked, all was clear, the brigade having moved off as fast as possible according to the orders received.

It was then near ten o'clock at night, very dark, and a large forest of many miles long to march through without a guide or companion, and the devils of wolves howling in all directions. About twelve or one o'clock I began to be very tired, when I saw a light glimmering at some distance, and making towards it I was glad on arriving to find an officer of the Rifle Corps in a hut, with some sick men and some baggage. I got some wine from him and a bit of something to eat, and lay down for half an hour, when I awoke and jumped up, and seizing my sword and cap I started off, having dreamt that my company was in action with the enemy; and I never halted till about eleven the next morning, when I overtook the brigade and marched on to '*Talavera's bloody field.*'

As we moved on, the road was crowded with cowardly fugitives—Spaniards innumerable, and lots of English, commissary clerks, paymasters, sutlers, and servants, to say nothing of a few soldiers and officers who said they were sick; all swearing the British Army was cut to pieces. How we did swear at them, and hiss every fellow we met! Moreover, these followers of the army were committing every kind of rascality and pillaging with impunity, as they never fail to do when out of reach of punishment. It is much more difficult to keep the civilians and followers of an army in order than twice, ay, ten times, the number of soldiers; the only way is to have plenty of provosts to hang and flog them without mercy, the devils incarnate. They disgrace an army more than anything.

At last our brigade arrived on the field of battle, after having marched *fifty miles in twenty-two hours*, every man having at least forty pounds weight upon his back! But our disappointment was great when we found we were too late, the battle having finished the night before. We took up the line of the advanced posts, and were employed burying the dead and saving the unfortunate wounded French from the fury of the Spanish peasants, who murdered them wherever they could find them without mercy. The field of battle was a horrid sight, particularly to us who had not shared either in the danger or the glory, though we did our best to arrive in time. The dry grass had caught fire, and numbers of wounded of all nations were burnt to death, being unable to crawl out of the way of the raging fire; then the dreadful smell from the half-burned carcases of the horses was appalling. In short, I never saw a field of battle which struck me with such horror as the field of Talavera.

In the course of a few days Lord Wellington's information of the movements of the French armies caused him to retire towards the Tagus; and as the bridge of Arzibispoa was some leagues in the rear, Lord Wellington made the Spaniards promise they would remain at Talavera and watch the movements of the enemy in their front, while he made the necessary arrangement for the British taking up a new position on the left bank of the Tagus, and prepared to meet Marshal Soult, who had reorganised his beaten army, and was moving down in full march on the rear of the British. Cuesta, the Spanish general, instead of remaining as he had promised Lord Wellington, the very moment the road was clear and that he knew our army was on the retreat, turned about and went off as fast as possible, leaving the British hospital at the mercy of the enemy, and of course the whole of our sick and wounded soldiers and officers were made prisoners by Marshal Victor, the French general-in-chief, who, immediately on learning that the English and Spaniards had evacuated the town, took possession of it. He behaved most kindly and generously to the wounded and the medical officers who were left in charge of the hospital.

We had just time to pass the Tagus by the bridge of Arzibispoa before Soult made his appearance, and the Light Brigade under General Craufurd was ordered to gain the bridge of Almaraz by a forced march, in order to prevent the French from crossing there and seizing the pass of Mirabete. This was done exactly as ordered, and the whole of Marshal Soult's plan of operations being frustrated (principally, however, by the jealousy of his brother marshals), Lord Wellington took up his headquarters at Deletoza. While the army remained in this position we suffered dreadfully from want of food; nothing but a small portion of unground wheat and (when we could *catch* them) about a quarter of a pound of old goats' flesh each man; no salt, bread, or wine; and as the Spaniards had plundered the baggage of the British Army during the Battle of Talavera, there was nothing of any kind to be procured to help us out, such as tea or sugar. Our brigade had to move down from a height every evening to watch the ford and bridge, and as the banks of the river were marshy we soon had enough of sickness.

At last Lord Wellington was determined to remain no longer in Spain or to co-operate with the Spanish armies and generals, as they were good for nothing in the field, and only marauded and insulted the British while inactive, so we received orders to march to the frontiers of Portugal. The headquarters were at Badajos, in Spain, and the rest of the army distributed in the various Portuguese towns along the frontier. The Light Brigade went to Campo Mayor, and never were poor fellows better pleased than we were to be under cover again and get good food, &c. I never in all my service felt so completely exhausted and worn out as at Almaraz, and it was there that I got the seeds of the ague which I suffered from for a full year afterwards. The hospital was established at Elvas, and there five or six thousand gallant British soldiers breathed their last. It was really dreadful to see the *dead cart* go round the town three times a day, loaded with dead bodies all naked, and tumbled into a hole outside the town, from whence the smell was horrid, notwithstanding all means were tried to prevent it.

In the course of a few months we moved towards the north of Portugal, and our regiment was quartered at a town called Piñhel. Some time afterwards we got orders to march into Spain, and were in cantonments along the banks of the river Aguada; the French under Marshal Ney being all round the neighbourhood of Ciudad Rodrigo. One night, the post occupied by the Rifle Corps was surprised, the enemy killing the sentry at the bridge and stealing unawares on the picket or advanced post. They were half-way up the bank or hill where the body of the regiment was, under Colonel Sidney Beckwith, before the alarm was given, and the regiment had only time to seize their arms and accoutrements, and ran out in their shirts, with their belts and cartouche boxes slung over them; and in this ridiculous dress, with old Beckwith at their head, in his dressing gown, red nightcap, and slippers, they fell upon the enemy and completely annihilated him, very few getting across the river again.

This was the first, and of course the last, surprise that any part of the Light Brigade ever had; for from that period to the battle of Toulouse no man in the army can say he ever saw a light division regiment negligent on its post; and in this instance of '*Barbe del Porco*' the Rifle Corps, which always was, and ever will be, one of the finest regiments in the service, made up by their gallantry and steadiness, and by well thrashing the enemy, for any little laxity of discipline which had occasioned the surprise, for surprise it was, there's no denying that.

One day I was on picket at a ford in front of the village of Gallejos, when I observed a general officer and his staff coming down the road on the opposite bank towards the ford. I called out across the river, which was narrow, to desire them to go back, and at the same time drew up my men and told the French general that I would fire at him if he persisted in coming down to the ford. They seemed to hold my threat in perfect contempt and still moved down; upon which I fired, and shot one of their horses. This had the desired effect, and they wheeled about and went back at a trot. The general, who was your Uncle Charles' old friend, Marshal Ney, rode a white horse; and as I was not aware at the time that it was he, I made my men do all they could to shoot him, as it is always a good thing to shoot your enemy's general, as it must make a great confusion in his army.

Another day, being on picket at the same place, where opposite to us the enemy had now also a picket, some of the French soldiers asked my leave to come across and get tobacco from our men, as they had none, and could not get any, in consequence of the siege. I allowed two of them to come, who immediately stripped off their clothes and swam across (for I would not let them try the ford), got the tobacco, told us all the news from France, and returned quite happy. Now this was all wrong, because, when a man is placed in charge of a post, he should never permit his enemy to come within reach of being able to observe what he is about, the strength of his party, or the nature of his defences. The safest plan is to keep him at a distance, and to allow of no familiarity or intercourse between your men and the enemy's.

No harm did happen by these men coming over to my picket, but there might have been danger from it, because the officer might have disguised himself as a private, and come over as such, and, being naked, I could not possibly tell him from a soldier; and when once over, he would have seen the strength of my post and the number of my men, and returned fully aware of all my weak parts of defence, and might have made some attempt during the night to surprise us.

You must never be slack in your duty, always active, looking out towards the enemy, visiting your sentinels, patrolling, never permitting your men and the enemy's to have any communication whatever; in short, when you are on guard, picket, or any duty, in the presence of the enemy, you must never sleep, but be eternally on the watch, particularly at night; and when you patrol (which you should always do a little beyond your furthest sentinel, and as near the enemy as possible, without danger of drawing a fire upon you, and by that means cause a false alarm), every now and then lay your ear to the ground and listen if you hear any noise like the movement of troops, or carriages, guns, &c., as it is surprising what a distance off you may of a still night hear the noise of the troops marching.

If there is any sound which you are not sure of, make some of your oldest soldiers listen also; and if still you are unable to make out the nature of the noise, immediately, but as silently as possible, order your men to stand to their arms, and so be prepared to do whatever may be necessary, either to fight or retreat, according to the orders you have received respecting the post. There is another thing you must *never* do, and that is drink one drop of wine or any strong liquor while upon duty. If you do, and it takes the least effect upon you, you are lost forever. Nothing can bring your character as an officer up again; you sink for the remainder of your life. No gallantry can bring you round; no man will ever be, or ought to be, trusted with the charge of a post or any number of men who gets drunk upon duty. Men are punished—either shot or flogged—for it, and no officer can escape being cashiered for it; besides, there can be no excuse.

Drunkenness is at all times ungentlemanlike and perfectly disgraceful; but there may perhaps, under certain circumstances, now and then be some slight excuse for it, but when on duty there can be none. The word 'duty' ought to act as a talisman, and, from the moment an officer is on duty, his whole thoughts, acts, and ideas should be bent upon the performance of it to the utmost of his abilities, and without respite till he is relieved and all responsibility off his shoulders; and as habit becomes second nature, an officer should train himself when at home and in peace to have the same activity and strict attention to his duty on guard as if it was in the face of an enemy; and then, when real service comes, he will have the habit so strong on him of unwearied attention to his duty, that he will never find himself at a loss, or be knocked up and fatigued, however severe may be the service required of him in face of an enemy.

Marshal Ney having taken the town of Ciudad Rodrigo after a

three weeks' siege and a gallant defence by the old Spanish governor, Lord Wellington thought it advisable to retreat slowly towards Portugal, being determined to keep pos-session of that country as long as possible; and as he is a man of most extraordinary firmness and transcendent abilities, he foresaw that under the existing circumstances of the Peninsula, and the immense numerical force of the French armies, which were well equipped and provided with everything necessary for a vigorous campaign, and the several corps commanded by Napoleon's best generals or marshals, it would be impossible for him to resist their combined attacks with so small a force as he had of good troops, more particularly now that the French emperor had placed Marshal Massena at the head of his army in Spain, so that the jealousy of the others towards each other, which had been the chief cause of their failure in many instances, was of little matter, as none of them dared to murmur against his orders, or act for themselves independently of him.

Lord Wellington, having well considered all this, determined upon one of those military and political movements which required the very greatest professional skill to execute, and the determined and powerful mind of a great man to adhere to—*viz.*, to retreat slowly upon Lisbon, and there make his stand and brave every effort of a daring and wily enemy, and the innumerable difficulties and embarrassments caused by the low and cunning intrigues of the base and vicious regency of Portugal. This he knew he must face; and also that his own government at home, assailed by the clamour and fears of a factious Opposition in Parliament, which was as presumptuous as it was ignorant of the powerful abilities of the extraordinary man who commanded the British Army, would not boldly and vigorously support him in his efforts to save Portugal from becoming a second time a prey to Napoleon's inordinate ambition and the military despotism of the French armies.

Lord Wellington having, as I said before, long foreseen that he would be forced to retreat, had early commenced his preparations for the security of his army when it should arrive at Lisbon, by making one of the strongest lines of defence possible, some leagues in front of Lisbon. This defence was called the 'Lines of Torres Vedras,' and consisted of redoubts and field-works of various kinds, according to the ground they were to defend, and all connected with each other by entrenchments, &c., so that, when occupied by the army, it would almost be impossible to force them. But, even supposing this first line of defence should be carried by the enemy, there was another, much more contracted, to retreat upon, where a very small force would hold out against the French Army and cover the embarkation of the British, should Lord Wellington be at last forced to quit Portugal.

I cannot help considering this retreat to the lines, and the pertinacity with which he held them in spite of every difficulty, and the remonstrances of the government at home, which was seized with alarm, as the, greatest proof of a master mind and genius that could be given, and proved Lord Wellington to be superior to any general the French had, except Napoleon; in short, that he was, next to Buonaparte himself, the first general of the day. And I am further convinced that, had he the same opportunities that Napoleon had, he would have proved as great a general, as his capacity and powers of mind would have strengthened and expanded in proportion to the vastness of his views and the obstacles to be surmounted.

But let me return to where I left off, with the account of this famous retreat. Upon the fall of the fortress of Ciudad Rodrigo we retreated towards Almeida, the frontier fortress of Portugal. One day a French captain of infantry with about one hundred and fifty or perhaps two hundred men was charged, by order of General Craufurd, by several squadrons of our cavalry, but without effect; for no impression was made upon his small force, as he reserved his fire till the cavalry were almost touching the points of his men's bayonets, and then poured a heavy fire upon them, which frightened the horses so much that it was impossible for the men to force them on, and they turned off and galloped away. This was repeated once or twice, and in the last charge made by the 14th Light Dragoons their commanding officer, poor Colonel Talbot, fell dead on the bayonets of the enemy.

General Craufurd then ordered a gun to be brought to bear upon this detachment of the French, and, at the same time, sent some riflemen down to drive them off, which had the desired effect; and this small intrepid band made good its retreat and escaped, after having behaved most gallantly and withstood the charges of several hundreds of our dragoons. The officer commanding had proved himself as skilful as he was brave, and every man who witnessed his conduct was delighted to see him escape. The fault was not in our cavalry, but in General Craufurd, who, upon seeing that the first charge of the dragoons made no impression, should have instantly sent a party of infantry, who would have settled the affair at once,, and saved the life of a gallant young officer of great promise, as well as the lives of the poor soldiers who fell a useless sacrifice to his obstinacy.

Nothing proves the steadiness of good infantry more than the manner in which they stand the repeated charges of cavalry; and it was to the persevering and steady cool conduct of the British infantry, who repulsed every charge of the French cavalry, that was mainly due the victory of Waterloo! But the Duke of Wellington knew the stern stuff his troops were made of, and feeling full reliance upon their steadiness and gallantry, he never, I believe, for one moment had a doubt of the result of that glorious day.

Your Uncle Charles went into the French Army with a flag of truce about some business a few hours after the affair I have related, and he had an opportunity of mentioning to the French general of division, Loisson, how gallantly and skilfully the captain and his little band had behaved, which pleased them very much. In a day or two we retreated towards the river Coa, which is a rapid river that runs behind the Portuguese frontier and the fortress of Almeida. During all this period I was suffering much from ague, which had continued for many months; still I never missed a day's duty or was a day absent from my company, which was very foolish, for had I gone to the rear and remained a few weeks in hospital, I most probably would have recovered, and been well and strong all the rest of the campaign; but the truth is, that to be obliged to go to the rear was what I never would consent to; and I believe I may without vanity say that few, if any, officers went less to the rear of the army than myself.

But sickness overcomes both body and mind of the strongest men, and it is harsh and cruel ever to blame or cast a slur on the soldier who is really ill. As to the *skulker*, if he is an officer, never have any mercy on him. Should he be a private soldier, reason with him, and endeavour to make him sensible of the shame and folly of his conduct before you attempt harsher means. Always bear in mind the difference between your situation as an officer and his as a private. You have every stimulus for exertion honours, rank, fame, comfort, and often pecuniary emolument; what has the soldier? nothing but the consciousness of having performed his duty, and that universal feeling among British soldiers, the glory of having upheld his country's character for bravery! But these are no substantial benefits, and of course he cannot be expected to have the same energy as his officer; for which reason that officer should never permit himself to hurt the feelings of a private by swearing at him or using harsh expressions.

Try every method before you resort to punishment—let that be the last; but when it is absolutely necessary, let it be inflicted with solemnity, and, as far as possible (if one may use the expression), with feeling. Punishment should always be considered as an *example* to deter others from the committal of crime, never as the means of inflicting torture upon the individual.

I revert so often to the subject of the punishment of soldiers because, although I am one of those who think, and after long consideration, that it would be impossible, as the army is at present instituted, to keep up the necessary discipline without corporal punishment, I am not an advocate for treating soldiers as if they were mere brutes, without either sense, feeling, or character. On the contrary, I have rarely met with a private soldier who had not feelings, and keen ones too; though often indeed they had been blunted by bad example and harsh treatment. Still, by perseverance and kindness, and letting them see that you look upon them as rational beings and as fellow-men, you will seldom fail to bring them back to their original dispositions. The officer who considers himself a better man than the private, except from his superior education and intelligence, is a presumptuous fool! For what would he be, or what could he do, without the private? Nothing! the fact being that upon the physical strength and moral courage of the British soldier mainly depends the success of our greatest generals.

And in many instances where the talents necessary to a great commander have been wanting, and all seemed lost, the determined gallantry and steadiness of the soldiers have turned the fate of the battle, and placed the laurel on a brow devoid of all military genius! So it is the *interest* as well as the moral duty of all officers to treat the men committed to their charge with every attention, kindness, justice, and *respect*, for that is no improper word. Although he is under his officer in rank, the private soldier is bound by the same ties to his country, has the same moral and natural affections as parent, husband, brother, or friend; is actuated and worked upon by the same passions and feelings, and worships the same great Author of our existence, who looks upon all, from the king to the beggar, with the same benevolence, and rewards each of us according to our deserts, without distinction of rank or birth.

Therefore I say the private soldier should be *respected* by his officer. I know this to be the opinion of the greatest, the best, and the wisest soldiers, and I can show you an order written by the Duke of Wellington when commander-in-chief of the army (after the Duke of York's death), in consequence of the punishment, in an irregular and disgraceful manner, of some soldiers in one of the regiments, by which you will perceive that the duke thinks in the same way as I do upon this subject; and *his* authority is worth all the opinions of those who imagine themselves so much wiser than others, and believe that being born gentlemen they have a right to treat those in a lower rank with insolence and contempt. The truly brave man is always merciful, so the true gentleman is neither proud nor insolent.

Before I return to the movements of the army, and while upon the subject of the private soldier, it is necessary to say that since Sir Henry Hardinge has been Secretary at War he has been busily and actively employed in bettering the condition of the soldier, and making regulations by which the private may by good conduct ensure to himself a comfortable pension upon which to retire when he has served for twenty years (*?twenty-one—Ed. W.N.*); and if forced to leave the service either from bad health or wounds, he will be certain of a just and proper provision, and not subject to the will or caprice of any man, as was formerly the case; many old and deserving soldiers who have been wounded having very small pensions, and others without wounds, and not half the number of years' service, receiving double the sum, to the great detriment of the country and injustice to the army.

But Sir Henry Hardinge has placed it all on a new and impartial footing, and I have no doubt if he is allowed to proceed in his own way he will in time regulate every branch of the service that comes under his control in such a manner that the *experiment* (for such it must be) of doing away with corporal punishment may be tried; but this must take a long time, and be done with the greatest caution, if ever accomplished. I shall now proceed with my narrative.

Combat of the Coa

One night, while in the neighbourhood of Almeida, I was very ill. It rained in torrents; the field where we bivouacked was newly ploughed, making it perfect mud, so that it was impossible to lie down. I suffered so much from a burning fever that the doctor and my brother Charles who was with me thought I would die. At last morning came: I was a little better, when suddenly we heard firing in our front, and in a short time we understood the enemy were advancing with their cavalry. This went on till at last our picquets were driven in, with a good deal of slaughter on our side, and a general and fierce attack made upon the brigade, particularly the 43rd and Rifle Corps, by the whole of Marshal Ney's corps of near twenty thousand men.

We were not much above four thousand including all arms, and, as the whole of the British Army except ourselves was several leagues in our rear on the other side of the river at Celerico, we could have no support; and more-over Lord Wellington had left General Craufurd merely to watch the enemy's motions and give him every information, while he had positively forbidden him to commit himself by any engagement, but to retreat, without firing a shot, upon the Almeida side of the river, Lord Wellington being well aware that the whole of the enemy's forces in the north of Spain had been concentrated under Marshal Massena for the invasion of Portugal, and that it would be only an unnecessary waste of lives to attempt any resistance till he had the whole allied army, joined by the greatest part of the Portuguese Militia, in position on the mountain of Busaco, where he had determined to await their attack.

Craufurd, however, let his vanity get the better of his judgement, and delayed so long that at last the enemy made a sudden attack, and it was with the utmost difficulty that the brigade made good its retreat over the bridge; indeed, some of the picquets were obliged to make the best of their way towards Almeida, and so got protection from the guns of the fortress, and moving down behind the town, crossed the river in the dusk of the evening as well as they could by swimming, and so joined us during the night. As soon as the regiments had passed the bridge, the 43rd, which was the last regiment, and the Rifle Corps were formed on the end of the bridge and on the ground and heights which commanded the passage, which was long and narrow; the artillery was so placed upon the high ground as to sweep the enemy's end of the bridge should they make the attempt to pass it; the 52nd Regiment was sent more to the right, in order to throw a flank fire upon the enemy, and also to be in reserve to support the other two regiments or cover their retreat, according to circumstances.

I was detached with my company to the right, close upon the edge of the river, to defend a part that was fordable. In a short time the enemy moved down a heavy column of infantry to force the passage over the bridge, but were received so steadily and gallantly by the 43rd and Rifle Regiments, that after three desperate attempts, and pushing better than half-way across, they gave up the point with great loss both in killed and wounded. We also suffered severely. My brother William was wounded in the hip in the last attack and effort to gain the bridge; his colonel and several other officers were killed. Where

I was the French only came half-way down to the bank of the river from the opposite height, and then a fine dashing fellow, a French staff officer, rode down just opposite my position to try if the river was fordable at that part. Not liking to fire at a single man I called out to him, and made signs that he must go back; but he would not, and being determined to try it, he dashed fearlessly into the water! It was then necessary to fire at him, and instantly both man and horse fell dead, and their corpses floated down the stream!

Thus perished a gallant fellow who had done his duty gloriously! And, strange as it may appear, we, his enemies, who had just put a period to his existence, heaved the sigh of pity for his fate, and many of us ejaculated 'What a pity! Poor fellow! God bless his soul!' This officer's death will to your young minds appear cruel and wanton on our part, or rather *mine*, who ordered him to be shot, but I had no option, because the object for which I was ordered to that post was to prevent the enemy passing at that part of the river which was considered fordable. The rain during the night had so swollen the river that the French were not sure that it was passable, and would not attempt the passage till an officer had been sent to try it.

Now, had I permitted the officer to cross and then made him a prisoner, it would have proved that the river could be forded, and of course a strong force would soon have crossed and obliged me to retreat, and at the same time have turned the position of the brigade on its right flank at the same moment that every effort was being made to force the passage of the bridge; and the result might and indeed would have been most disastrous to the whole brigade; therefore it was absolutely necessary that I should prevent his getting beyond a few yards into the water, and the only means I had in my power to do so was by ordering the men to shoot him, poor fellow! and his horse also, for had the animal crossed without his rider it would have served the enemy's purpose just the same, so the poor horse was shot.

One of the great evils of war is that many very harsh and, to appearance, cruel acts must be done to individuals for the general good, or rather, I should say, to ensure success on one side or other, the *good* being very little that is done by war, so seldom is it carried on for the defence of the weak or the liberties of mankind! And I fear it is vain to expect the world to control its passions and vices in such manner that universal peace may reign over the earth; but it is every man's duty to exert himself in his station, and particularly that of officers, to ameliorate, as far as is in his power, the dreadful horrors and scourge of war!

Little, very little, do those who have only *read* of war know the sufferings of those countries where armies are opposed to each other.

As I have already said, the enemy being repulsed at all points the firing ceased, and as soon as it was completely dark the brigade moved silently off and pursued its retreat upon Celerico. The French did not immediately follow us, and when we halted and formed our bivouac, Charles and I went into Celerico to see what had become of our brother William and our friend Captain Lloyd, of the 43rd, who had likewise received a wound. He was one of the finest fellows in the British army, and, had he been permitted to live, would have distinguished himself as much as any officer in that army.

Indeed, at the period he was killed, he had risen to the rank of lieutenant-colonel commanding a regiment, by his own merit and the judicious employment of his uncommon talents in every branch of the military art—drawing, surveying, fortification, languages, geography—and his perfect knowledge of all outpost duties, and the interior details necessary to be thoroughly acquainted with as a commanding officer of a regiment; in short, when poor Lloyd fell so gloriously as he did at the head of his regiment, the 94th, every man in the British Army regretted him as one whose early fame gave a promise of future greatness which few obtain. But it was otherwise ordained, and Lloyd fell ere the fruit of glory and renown had reached full maturity.

When we arrived at Celerico, we found them not dangerously but severely wounded, and settled in the Spanish General Alava's quarters, who was then *aide-de-camp* to Lord Wellington. He had seen these two English officers brought into the town on a bullock car, dreadfully jolted, and a burning sun blazing over their heads; and although the place was headquarters and full of British officers of every description, all of whom had good, comfortable quarters, and were idling about, not a soul offered to take them in, or to go and look for a house for them, and they lay in the cart for many hours without shade or water or any notice taken of them. Not even did a surgeon go near them; and as Lord Wellington and his staff were away in front, they did not see them.

Had he been in the town they would not have dared to leave the wounded for hours in this shameful state of neglect and misery, for I must say that I never saw any officers of Lord Wellington's personal staff who were not ever ready to be of use to the sick and wounded, and to exert themselves in every way to make them comfortable and to show them every real kindness; though I acknowledge *some* of them had not the most polite or conciliating manners when a dinner was given at headquarters to *regimental* officers. But there were three great exceptions to this—namely, Lord March (the present Duke of Richmond), Lord Fitzroy Somerset, and the present Lord Downe (then Colonel Burgh).

As to Lord Fitzroy Somerset, he has carried his popularity with him through every situation he has held since he entered the army to the present moment (1828), in which he is military secretary to the commander-in-chief, and where I hope he may long continue, the supporter and patron of every good soldier. He has already done more good to the army in his situation than all his predecessors put together, because he has a more thorough knowledge of the army and its officers than almost any man I know; indeed, I do not know the man who could equal him in his situation, for which he has every requisite.

But to return to William and his friend. General Alava, seeing the neglect with which they were treated, went and offered them his house, and there every comfort he had was given to them with that frankness and kind-heartedness which so highly distinguished that gallant and noble-minded Spaniard, who, from that time to the present period, has always been our friend. He took part in the revolution in Spain in 1820, and since that has been obliged to live in England and France, having been driven from his country, for which he fought and bled for years, a wandering exile, his property confiscated, and his constitution broken down by hard service and mental misery at seeing the unhappy state into which his beloved country has been plunged by the cowardly, cruel, and contemptible Ferdinand!

To the honour of the Duke of Wellington, the moment he heard of Alava's misfortunes, and that he had made his escape and was at Gibraltar, he wrote to him to say that as long as he lived he should provide for him; that he should have apartments in his house in London, and never feel the loss of property in a pecuniary point of view; he also gave him a small house in the park of Strathfieldsaye. This was very right and kind on the duke's part, and General Alava was fully sensible of it; but after a year or two he found his health would not stand the damp and cold of our climate, and he went to Tours, in France, where he resides upon the interest of a few thousand pounds which luckily he had placed in the British funds when he was ambassador at Brussels and Paris. He told me he had about two hundred a year, and, having that, he refused all relief from our government or that of France.

Battle of Busaco

In the course of a short time the army retreated towards Busaco. As our brigade formed the rearguard we were continually in conflict with the enemy's advance, but as we generally kept at a respectable distance from each other, but few men were killed and wounded, and two or three officers at most. Every night I suffered from fever or ague during this retreat; but what is very curious r as showing the effect the mind has upon the body, the moment we engaged with the enemy the ague left me, and I was quite strong and able to do my duty, and go through my day's work as well as any officer in the regiment, without the least feeling of illness or weakness; but when we halted at night I lost all energy, and was as suffering and miserable a wretch as can well be conceived.

At length we arrived at the heights of Busaco, a range of mountains very high, and in parts very steep and difficult of access. There was a convent of the order of La Trappe on the top, but some distance in the rear of the position. At this convent Lord Wellington took up his quarters, and disposed his army in position to fight a battle if the enemy had the boldness—indeed I might say the temerity—to attack him. Lord Hill's (then General Hill) corps was on our right, the 3rd (General Picton's) division and the 1st division were in the centre, the Light Brigade on their left, and General Cole, with the 4th division, quite on the left flank of the whole. The Portuguese regular troops were mixed with our divisions, and a second line was formed of the militia and armed peasantry.

I should suppose the whole force under the Duke of Wellington was about sixty-five or seventy thousand men,[2] and the position itself was by nature as strong as possible, so that it appeared to all of us that Marshal Massena would never attempt to carry it; and if he did make the attempt, we were perfectly certain he would be driven back and repulsed with great slaughter. We remained in position one day, during which time the various divisions and brigades were employed in getting everything in order, so that when the enemy did come on he should have enough of it.

The morning of the second day we perceived a movement in the enemy's camp, which was on the heights opposite us, a small stream running through the valley which divided the armies. We judged their force to be nearly equal to ours—certainly Massena could not have

---

2. Fifty thousand, according to Napier.—Ed. (W.N.)

had less than sixty thousand men in his camp—so that about one hundred and thirty thousand men were going to have a fierce and bloody struggle with each other; the forces of the two armies nearly equal in point of numbers, but not so in composition, as the enemy's was composed of the finest soldiers of France, none of whom that could not count many years of hard-fought campaigns, and had gained numerous victories and in various countries; in short, a finer army or better appointed could not be well conceived, and at its head was Marshal Massena, then looked upon as next to Napoleon himself in military fame.

Our army was, on the contrary, composed of bad and inexperienced troops as well as good and experienced ones, for Lord Wellington had not above thirty thousand real soldiers, the rest were raw and undisciplined Militia, who had never seen a shot fired or an enemy in battle array before; so that upon the British soldiers he depended for the successful issue of the fight, and gloriously did they prove themselves worthy of his confidence. The French had now formed their columns and were moving steadily and gallantly down to the valley below in three bodies, meaning to attack and penetrate our line at three different points—*viz.* the right, centre, and left, where our division (for we had been formed into two brigades, having had two Portuguese regiments incorporated with us, under the command of Colonels Beckwith, Rifle Corps, and Barclay, 52nd Regiment) was stationed on the steepest part of the mountain.

We were retired a few yards from the brow of the hill, so that our line was concealed from the view of the enemy as they advanced up the heights, and our skirmishers retired, keeping up a constant and well-directed running fire upon them; and the brigade of horse artillery under Captain Hugh Ross threw such a heavy fire of shrapnel-shells, and so quick, that their column, which consisted of about eight thousand men, was put into a good deal of confusion and lost great numbers before it arrived at a ledge of ground just under the brow of the hill, where they halted a few moments to take breath, the head of the column being exactly fronting my company, which was the right company of our brigade, and joining the left company of the 43rd, where my brother William was with his company.

General Craufurd himself stood on the brow of the hill watching every movement of the attacking column, and when all our skirmishers had passed by and joined their respective corps, and the head of the enemy's column was within *a very few yards of him*, he turned round, came up to the 52nd, and called out, 'Now, 52nd, revenge the death of Sir John Moore! Charge, charge! Huzza!' and waving his hat in the air he was answered by a shout that appalled the enemy, and in one instant the brow of the hill bristled with two thousand British bayonets wielded by steady English hands, which soon buried them in the bodies of the fiery Gaul!

My company met the head of the French column, and immediately calling to my men to form column of sections in order to give more force to our rush, we dashed forward; and as I was by this movement in front of my men a yard or two, a French soldier made a plunge at me with his bayonet, and at the same time his musket going off I received the contents just under my hip and fell. At the same instant the French fired upon my front section, consisting of about nine men in the front rank, *all of whom* fell, four of them dead, the rest wounded, so that most probably by my being a little advanced in front my life was saved, as the men killed were exactly those nearest to me. Poor Colonel Barclay also received a severe wound (of which he afterwards died in England). I got upon my legs immediately again and pursued the enemy down the hill, for by this time they had been completely repulsed, and were running away as fast as their legs could carry them.

William and his friend Captain Lloyd, who were upon my right, seeing that the French were still in column and in great confusion from the unexpected suddenness of the charge and the shout which accompanied it, had wheeled up their companies by the left, and thus flanked the French column and poured a well-directed fire right into them. Major Arbuthnott, who was on my left, did the same with the remaining companies of the 52nd, so that the enemy was beset on both flanks of his column, and, as you may suppose, the slaughter was great. We kept firing and bayoneting till we reached the bottom, and the enemy passed the brook and fell back upon their main body, which moved down to support them and cover their retreat. All this was done in a very short time—that is, it was not above twenty minutes from the charge till the French were driven from the top to the bottom of the mountain like a parcel of sheep. I really did not think it was possible for such a column to be so completely destroyed in a few minutes as that was, particularly after witnessing how gallantly they moved up under a destructive fire from the artillery and a constant galling one from our sharpshooters.

We took some prisoners, and among them General Simon, a gallant officer, but a bad and a dishonourable man, who afterwards broke his parole of honour. He was horribly wounded in the face, his jaw being broken and almost hanging down on his chest. Just as myself and another officer came to him, a soldier was going to put his bayonet into him, which we prevented, and sent him a prisoner to the general. As I went down the hill following the enemy, I saw seven or eight French officers lying wounded. One of them as I passed caught hold of my little silver canteen and implored me to stop and give him a drink, but, much as it pained me to refuse, I could not do it, being in full pursuit of the enemy, and it was impossible to stop for an instant.

This may be thought hard-hearted, but in war we often do and *must* do many harsh and unfeeling things. Had I stopped to give him a drink I must have done so for the others, and then I should have been the last at the bottom of the hill instead of one of the first in pursuit of the enemy; and recollect, my boys, that an officer should always be *first* in advancing against the enemy and *last* in retreating from him. When we got to the bottom, where a small stream ran between us and the enemy's position, by general consent we all mingled together searching for the wounded. During this cessation of fighting we spoke to each other as though we were the greatest friends and without the least animosity or angry feeling!

One poor German officer in the French Army came to make inquiries respecting his brother, who was in our service in the 60th Regiment, which was at that time composed principally of foreigners, and upon looking about he found him dead, the poor fellow having been killed. Very soon Lord Wellington, finding we remained as he thought too long below, ordered the bugles to sound the retreat, and the French general having done the same, off scampered the soldiers of each army and returned to their several positions like a parcel of schoolboys called in from play by their master.

I was so stiff by this time that I had difficulty in walking up the hill again and was obliged to get Mr. Winterbottom, the adjutant of the regiment, to help me up. When I arrived at the top, I understood that my brother Charles was severely wounded in the face while attending Lord Wellington during the battle, and that he was gone, or rather carried, to the rear, attended by our cousin Captain Charles Napier of the navy, who had been with us for some weeks as an amateur, not having a ship at that time and being too active and enterprising a fellow to remain at home idle waiting for one. He had gone out with me the evening before the battle to skirmish a little with the French pickets, as General Craufurd thought they had advanced rather closer to the foot of our position than was right, so I was ordered to move down and push them a little farther off.

Charles Napier our cousin *would* take a little white pony I had, to ride with us, notwithstanding I told him it was very foolish for most certainly he would get hit, being the only person on horseback. But he chose to go his own way and in less than half an hour he got shot in the calf of the leg, but very slightly; and I was delighted at it, the obstinate dog, he deserved it well! However, he was very good-humoured and laughed as much as anyone at his own folly. William had escaped being wounded in the battle and he and I were very glad to find ourselves side by side again.

In about half an hour after we returned to our position the whole army was under arms and Lord Wellington rode along the line receiving a cheer from every regiment as he passed. While in the act of doing this I am sorry to say the French general did a most unhandsome thing, and that was to make one of his batteries fire at Lord Wellington as he rode along accompanied by his staff! This was shameful and cowardly, because Marshal Massena knew (the thing was too evident for him not to know) that he was only reviewing and thanking his troops for their bravery, and he should have prevented any such act. Had Marshal Soult or Marshal Ney been the general in command of the French Army they would have scorned such an act.

We remained the rest of that day and the one following in the position, expecting a fresh attack from the enemy; but Marshal Massena had enough of it, and the second day after the action our army silently moved off before daybreak on. the road to Coimbra, leaving our fires and pickets, the latter retreating also as soon as daylight came. Our division as usual formed the rearguard and as we were passing by the Convent of La Trappe General Craufurd ordered me to post myself in the garden of it, which overlooked the late position of the army and commanded the road by which the troops were retiring, and there to remain and defend it as long as I had a man left!

This I should have done, for I was determined to keep my post if I lived as long as I had a cartridge left to load with; but as no enemy appeared I had no opportunity of showing what good stuff an English company of light infantry was made of. It was ascertained in about an hour that the enemy had moved off also and were marching by another road to Coimbra, which they expected to reach before us and so cut off the British army, or at least a large portion of it, from the retreat to the lines.

We arrived some hours sooner than the French at Coimbra, from which Lord Wellington had ordered all the inhabitants to withdraw and carry all their property and provisions with them; but as they had unfortunately delayed doing this till we were actually on the march through the town, the hurry, fright, and confusion were beyond description, and I never witnessed so heart-rending a scene! Beautiful women and young children, the aged, the decrepit, the sick, the poor, the rich, nobles and peasants, all in one dense mass of misery, wretchedness, and confusion; some barefoot, others crying, women tearing their hair with loud lamentations, and calling on every saint in the calendar, many of them running to the officers for protection and food, the weather bad, and all drenched with rain; and, to crown all, when we who were the last of the troops were passing by the prison, which was also the madhouse, the unfortunate inmates, prisoners and maniacs, were all at the grated windows rending the air with wild shrieks of despair at seeing the whole population of the city driven before us through the gate, and these unfortunate wretched creatures all locked in, and a fire having broken out in some houses close by them which they with reason expected every moment to communicate with the prison, and that they must all perish in the flames!

The British officers and soldiers could not stand this sight, and we soon broke open the gates and let them all loose; the maniac, the murderer, and the thief were turned adrift without a moment's hesitation or an instant's; thought, by which many a villain of the deepest dye was again let loose upon society and escaped the punishment due to his crimes. But what else was to be done? We had no time to make inquiries, their keepers or jailers had left them, the flames were fast approaching, and the enemy entering the town! If we did wrong, it was from motives of humanity and under circumstances that those only who were present can appreciate, and I feel confident that no man of feeling could for one moment blame us.

As we moved along, driving this immense multitude of unhappy people before us, houseless, penniless, and hungry, I could not help cursing war and all its dreadful attributes, and inwardly feeling that I was myself one of the instruments by which so much misery and injustice was inflicted on a poor guiltless race of inoffensive human beings, not one of whom most probably ever had a voice in the decision of peace or war, and who were scourged so severely, for what?—the inordinate ambition and personal aggrandisement of a ruthless soldier,

Napoleon Buonaparte! Much as I admire that most extraordinary man as a warrior, and splendid as were his talents in all things, I can never look back to his deeply cunning and treacherous invasion of Spain and Portugal, the crimes and horrors which in consequence were committed, the seas of blood which flowed, and the absolute misery of millions of a harmless population, without condemning him.

About the third day's march I was so ill and stiff with my wound that I could no longer sit my horse, and was forced to get into a cart and make the best of my way to Lisbon, in the progress of which one cold, dark, rainy night the Portuguese driver decamped and left his cart and myself sticking in the mud. Seeing a light at some distance I got out of the cart and made my way to it, but was so exhausted with pain and illness (having the ague also) that I sank down perfectly done up at the door of the house from whence the light had proceeded.

And luckily for me this was the quarter of my friend Sir Lowry Cole, commanding the 4th division, who, upon being informed that a wounded officer was at his door, instantly came out, had me carried in, gave me his own bed, had a surgeon sent for to dress my wound (the same who afterwards cut off my arm), and then sent me a good dinner; after which I fell asleep, and awoke next morning at daybreak quite refreshed and able to get on with General Cole's staff to the lines, where I took my leave of my kind friend the general, whose kindness to me I can never forget or cease to be most grateful for as long as I live. But I am not a solitary instance of Sir Lowry Cole's kindness and generosity, for he never would permit officer or *private soldier* to want anything that he had, or that it was in his power to procure for him; and though a hot-tempered man, he is as kind and generous as he is brave, and a more truly gallant, enterprising soldier never breathed.

From the lines I went to Lisbon, which was so crammed with troops, sick and wounded soldiers, commissaries and their clerks, all the skulkers and riff-raff of the army, besides thousands of Portuguese driven in from the country towns, that it was hardly possible to get a place to lodge in. But good luck attended me here also, for by accident I found the house where my brother Charles was quartered and who had arrived some days before, having suffered much from the pain of his wound (which was very severe) and the great neglect of the medical men, who seemed to have troubled themselves very little about him or any of the wounded, being more anxious to take care of themselves than to perform their duty to the sick and wounded.

But I must say that those medical men whom, unfortunately for him, he came under were all young men just arrived from England, many of them both idle and ignorant; and from the circumstance of the army being on the retreat and closely followed by the enemy, these young surgeons had nobody to give them orders or teach them their duty as military men, so that they were completely left to themselves, which is some excuse for their conduct. And I am bound to state that if one takes the conduct of the whole medical department of the army during the Peninsular War into consideration, one will find few such large bodies of men who are more distinguished for their kindness, skill, and indefatigable exertions for the health and comfort of the sick and wounded; and, as to danger, the medical officers of the British Army without exception have invariably shown an utter contempt for it, and in the execution of their duty will brave death, either in the field of battle or, which requires a higher mental courage, in the hospitals of the plague and yellow fever!

I am more particular upon this subject because it is a very general, but a very erroneous and unjust, idea in the army to think slightly of the medical men and to consider their profession as inferior to others, which is a great mistake, for few officers receive so good an education or are so generally acquainted with science and literature; and although I confess one does sometimes meet a ridiculous puppy of an assistant surgeon, or hospital mate, or even a pompous coxcomb in the higher departments, yet (and I speak from thirty years' experience) I never met anything but kindness, generosity, and manly, honourable conduct, combined with skill and judgement, in those medical gentlemen with whom I have served; and you will generally find the surgeon of your regiment a man whose society will be agreeable to you, and whose information, opinions, and experience will be of much benefit to you.

I only wish they were better off in pecuniary circumstances, for when I consider the great expense of their education, which they cannot avoid, and the length of time before they obtain the rank of surgeon of a regiment, or staff-surgeon, the pay they receive is very inadequate to their deserts, and not equal to what they would most probably have made in private practice, particularly where they have very distinguished abilities. Some of my greatest friends, and men for whom I have the highest esteem and respect, are in the medical department of the army.

I found Charles in bed very ill, his face so dreadfully swollen that I could neither see eyes nor nose, and having only heard that 'he was dreadfully wounded in the face' when I beheld him this horrid-looking figure, I really thought his nose had been shot off! And as you are aware what a fine long one he has, you can easily imagine how swollen his face must have been to hide it! The ball had entered on one side of his nose and passing through had lodged in the jawbone of the opposite side, from whence it was abstracted with much difficulty, great part of the jaw coming away with it as well as several teeth.

During this long and painful operation he never uttered a word or winced while under the surgeon's hands who performed the operation, and who told me he never saw a man who bore pain so patiently and manfully, and I hope, boys, you will do the same when your time comes to be wounded! though I must confess I did not bear the amputation of my arm as well as I ought to have done, for I made noise enough when the knife cut through my skin and flesh. It is no joke I assure you, but still it was a shame to say a word, and is of no use.

The French lady in whose house I found my brother was a very kind, excellent, clever, dirty, snuffy little old woman, who insisted on my taking up my quarters in her house, and she was as kind to us as possible then and ever afterwards. Her name was Madame Frannalette; her husband had been a merchant, but was dead, and because she was a Frenchwoman the Portuguese Government was distrustful of her and treated her very harshly in many instances, but being French her gaiety was incessant, whether ill-treated or well-treated—*toujours gaie.* In this house we gradually recovered from our wounds, and used to be merry and happy enough, having many friends who came to see us and often dined with us, particularly when business or duty brought any of our brother officers into Lisbon they were sure to come to us.

Opposite to our lodgings were some very pretty young ladies whom we wished to get acquainted with, but as their friends did not much like the English officers these girls told us across the street (which was very high and exceedingly narrow) that if we wished to visit them we must get across the street from our window in at theirs (as we would not be allowed to go in by the street-door) and then they would be happy to entertain us and give us some tea and coffee. Now in saying this jokingly these young ladies never had an idea that we would attempt such a thing, as our windows were in the third storey and at least thirty or forty feet from the ground; but they forgot they had young Englishmen to deal with, so as soon as it was dusk, and the people walking in the street below could not readily distinguish us, we procured some very long planks, and tying them together so as to reach the opposite window we rested one end on theirs and fastening the other firmly on our own we ran across and jumped into their room to their utter astonishment; however as we had performed our part they very graciously and most good-humouredly performed theirs by giving us coffee and cake, and we had a merry evening, laughing and talking bad Portuguese, to the amusement of the young ladies.

However, we were requested not to perform the same feat again, to which we assented upon condition that we should be permitted to repeat our visit in a proper manner through the doorway and up the stairs, which being agreed upon we often paid a visit and were introduced to their parents and friends and found other young ladies invited to meet us. Now all this was very agreeable and amusing, as abroad they do not mind these things so much, but such an adventure could never happen in England as our manners and ideas of society would not permit such a thing being even thought of, much less put in practice.

About this time a very great friend of ours, Captain Packenham of the navy, who always used to be of our parties to the young ladies, was appointed to a ship and came to dine with us, and in talking over his going home to join his ship he said, 'Well, I care not where I am sent so that it is not to cruise in Lough-Swilly Bay on the Irish Coast, for if I go there I am sure I shall be lost.' We of course laughed at him, but I never shall forget with what a serious and melancholy expression of countenance he held to his opinion. When he arrived in England he found the ship was ordered to the very place he dreaded, and in a few weeks after her arrival in the bay a storm arose and she went down, and not a soul left to tell the melancholy tale! His body was drifted ashore and buried with hundreds of his unfortunate crew. Poor Packenham! a gayer or more kind-hearted fellow never wore a blue coat.

CHAPTER 4

Advance from the Lines of Torres Vedras

But to return to the operations in front of the Lines of Torres Vedras. In consequence of the French not finding provisions or the towns inhabited as they expected, it was with the utmost difficulty that Marshal Massena could support his army in front of the lines for some weeks, and he was at last forced to retreat to the town and district of Santarem, where he took up a strong position and fortified his camp, being obliged in his turn to act upon the defensive, for Lord Wellington immediately followed him and took up a position opposite the enemy's front, who, being thus baffled in his attempt to carry our lines and drive us into the sea, as Napoleon had boasted he would do, was forced to be content to remain at Santarem in hopes of our being obliged to embark for want of means of subsistence, or that the English nation, tired and burdened with the expense of supporting an army in Portugal, would at last force the ministry to recall Lord Wellington and his army.

But here again Napoleon was baffled, both in his estimation of the character of the English nation and the intrepid firmness and military skill of the British general, who had long before calculated his means and determined upon his plans, from which he never deviated, and to which must be attributed the ultimate expulsion of the French from the Peninsula, and the glorious march of the Anglo-Portuguese army under its great commander from Lisbon to France, and finishing with the hard-fought battle and splendid victory of Toulouse.

At this time I went to rejoin my regiment, which was in advance, quartered in some of the villages in front of the enemy's position of Santarem, our right resting on the Tagus with a small stream in our front, rather deep, beyond which was a marshy plain. There were two bridges over this little river, with a long causeway leading from one of them, over which was the road to Santarem. These two bridges were about half a mile or less from each other, and a company was posted at each to watch them, with orders that should the enemy attempt to force the passage to fire the mines and blow up the bridges, as everything was prepared for that purpose by the engineers. My company was posted at the lower one on the right, which was not that over which the great road passed, but there was a private road which led through the marsh to the enemy's position.

One night, between twelve and one o'clock, I was visiting my sentinels and post in order to be sure all was quiet before I lay down to sleep, when suddenly I heard a shot, then another, and the noise of men as if coming down on our post. It was so pitch dark I could see nothing, and I was just going to blow, up the bridge when I thought I would first venture a little way beyond on the enemy's side and listen if I could hear the noise of men marching, and be quite satisfied before I set fire to the mine. My company was drawn up in three minutes across our end of the bridge and I went over to the other side with two or three men, and placing our ears to the ground we listened attentively for a few minutes, when I felt assured there was no enemy approaching; and therefore bringing up an officer and ten men, I ordered him to remain there, and if the enemy should advance upon him to fire and instantly retreat as hard as he and his men could run across the bridge, as I should be ready the instant he passed to blow it up.

While I was giving the orders we heard several more shots from the left near the other bridge, but I perceived by the flash that they came from our side of the stream; and we also saw and heard many splashes of water, as if people were crossing the river; and at that moment a sergeant came to tell me that the Brunswick Oels Corps (which was principally composed of deserters and French soldiers, who had enlisted into that regiment rather than remain in the Spanish hulks at Cadiz, where they had been cruelly treated by the Spaniards) was deserting, and that I was to fire upon them and take as many prisoners as I could. I therefore sent some of my men on one side and some on the other, and we soon found these poor fellows swimming across. We were obliged to fire at some of them who had got over and were getting off to the enemy, and a great number were killed.

However, as soon as daylight came, the greatest part were taken, and the rest returned to their quarters. Next day Lord Wellington ordered seventeen (I think) of them to be tried, all of whom were sentenced to be shot as deserters to the enemy; but he only executed five of them, and these, being Frenchmen, were much to be pitied, as they were taken prisoners at the time of Dupont's surrender, and if the Spaniards had not refused most shamefully to put the terms of capitulation into execution these unfortunate men would have been sent back to France. The British Government did all in its power to get the soldiers of Dupont's army released from their horrible confinement and treatment, but to no purpose; and, as a last resource, they offered to take them into our service if they would enlist, which they immediately did, as by that means they became British soldiers and were claimed by our government as such.[1]

These men were sent to the different foreign regiments in our service, and a considerable number came out and joined the Brunswick Oels Corps, then in the Light Division. Being close to the position of their countrymen, and every day seeing their former regiments and comrades within almost speaking distance of them, they were unable to resist the temptation of crossing the little river and being in half an hour among their countrymen, and once more wearing the tricolour cockade and fighting under their national flag.

When led out for execution they requested not to be tied to the stakes, and one of them, who had been a '*sous-officier*' in his own service, addressed his comrades who were drawn up to witness the execution, saying:

> I know that by the laws of the service I am now in I deserve death, because desertion to the enemy is so punished in the English Army; but I have been brought up in different notions, therefore it is no moral crime upon my part, who am not an Englishman but a German (Alsace). I have no fear of death, and am prepared to enter the presence of my Maker, being unconscious of having offended Him. I was compelled to enter the British service in order to escape the cruelty of the Spaniards, who had unlawfully kept me a prisoner contrary to the capitulation, and can it be wondered at, or can it be considered a crime that, when opposite my own countrymen and in daily sight of my old comrades, I should try to join them and once more fight under the colours of France? No, comrades! You

---

1. Why did not our government then send them back to France instead of sending them to fight their countrymen?—Ed. (W.N.)

who know me will consider me guiltless, and, like me, glory in death! When the English bullets have penetrated my breast, dip my handkerchief in my blood and distribute it among you as a relic of my devotion to France.

He then knelt down with the others in front of his grave, which in a military execution is always dug ready to receive the body of the culprit, and on the word being given to the party to fire, he and his unfortunate companions fell, but not dead (which sometimes happens, though very rarely), and he rose again and would have addressed the soldiers, had not a fresh party instantly stepped close up to these poor fellows and put a period to their existence by blowing out their brains. This fine fellow, for such he undoubtedly was, spoke in German, being an Alsacian, so that I may not have stated exactly all he said or the precise words he used, as the officer who told me, although he understood German, was not sufficiently master of the language to give a perfectly correct translation of the speech, but he said that as near as he could make out at the distance he was from him the above was the purport of it.

When he was dead those whom he addressed ran forward and tearing off the handkerchiefs with which the poor victim's eyes had been bound, pressed them to the wounds, and when all wet with the blood of their dead comrade, tore them in pieces and distributed them among one another. We all lamented the fate of these poor brave fellows at the time, and thought it was a very harsh thing to shoot them; but upon consideration I do not see how Lord Wellington could well have pardoned them, desertion among the foreign troops in our service having reached a considerable height, and it was only a few days before that Lord Wellington had pardoned several of them and issued an order stating his determination not to pardon in future any soldier caught attempting to desert to the enemy, no matter what his previous character might have been; and he warned all the foreign soldiers particularly that they must not expect any mercy, for they would be invariably shot in twenty-four hours after they were taken.

And indeed it was absolutely necessary, for all these deserters carried their arms and accoutrements with them, and gave much valuable information to the enemy of our strength, movements, and position, as well as of the number of foreign troops we had, and where these troops were placed, most of whom only waited for favourable opportunities to go over to the enemy. Of course, if they found that they were pardoned when taken in the attempt to desert, they would try again on the first opportunity.

Lord Wellington was placed in a very critical situation, and often found it necessary to be stern and inflexible in his administration of the army; and I am sure, though he is not a man who outwardly shows any softness of feeling, that he has always felt the greatest repugnance to ordering military executions or harsh treatment of either officers, soldiers, or inhabitants. You may have remarked that I often state this, for I think the Duke of Wellington does not get the credit which is his due upon the score of feeling, He has a short manner of speaking and a stern look, which people mistake for want of heart; but I have witnessed his kindness to others, and felt it myself in so many instances and so strongly, that I cannot bear to hear him accused of wanting what I know he possesses; as he has, by his own transcendent abilities, risen to the highest power and rank that a British subject can attain, so will there be found people always ready to detract from his merit, and try every means to sink him in public opinion, but I am confident that his manly and straightforward character will foil all such base attempts.

But to return to my narrative. I think it was about the 4th of March, at daybreak, that we perceived the enemy had withdrawn his advance pickets, and immediately upon its being reported to Lord Wellington, the whole British Army was in movement, pursuing Marshal Massena, who, finding himself unable from total want of provisions to maintain himself longer in his position, had commenced his memorable retreat from Portugal, thus proving Lord Wellington correct in his calculations, who had by his retreat to the lines and his resolute defence of them saved Portugal; for I believe he received many despatches from the ministers in England, proposing that he should abandon Portugal and embark with the army for England; and to him, and *him alone*, was due the ultimate evacuation of the Peninsula by the French.

We followed the enemy closely, being the advanced guard, and everywhere found proofs of the starving condition they were reduced to, and the severe privations they must have endured. Certainly Marshal Massena, as a general, deserves the greatest credit for having kept his army in position so long under such harassing circumstances and the great discontent that prevailed in his army; but then we must look on the other side also, and see what misery and destruction he caused to those unfortunate inhabitants who did not get away as ordered by Lord Wellington, or who fled into the hills in the false idea that in a few days the French would either be masters of Lisbon, having forced us to embark, or. failing in that, would have marched back again to Spain. These wretched people, to the amount of thousands, had every article of furniture and food taken from them, and starved by hundreds daily! A French officer who was made prisoner during this retreat, and to whom I had it in my power to be kind, told me that after a few weeks from their first arrival at the lines an order was given by Massena that every captain must provide his company with provisions in the best manner he could, which was generally done as follows.

A captain and his company went off into the country, and on coming to a peasant's hut or cabin he demanded provisions, upon which the miserable father and his wife and half-starving children went down on their knees supplicating the officer not to take the miserable pittance they had left for their sole support. But this had no effect, and the father was told that he should be hung up to a beam; and if he made a sign, that was agreed upon, that he would show where all his provisions were concealed, he would be instantly cut down, but if not, there he would hang till dead. Well, the wretched man, looking at his starving wife and helpless children, would determine on dying rather than tell where the little he had for their existence was hid. He was hung up accordingly, when in a few seconds the natural love of life and the shrieks of his distracted wife and children overcame the resolution to die. He gives the signal, is cut down, recovers his senses, and points out, with despair depicted in his haggard countenance, the spot where all he has to keep life in his wife and children is deposited, and he sees the ruthless plunderers depart without sparing him one morsel.

But is this all? No! In a few hours afterwards comes a fresh party of soldiers in search of provisions, and finds this unfortunate family nearly exhausted, but will give no credit to their story of what had already taken place sometime before, but instantly resort to the same barbarous measure of hanging up the father, who again, urged by the hopes of preserving his life a few minutes longer, makes the preconcerted signal. But, alas! when cut down, not being able to produce what has already been the prey of former robbers, is seized by the merciless soldiers and either shot or hanged, with the certainty that his miserable wife and children must perish with hunger. The French officer who told me this said it had often happened to him to witness such scenes during the stay of Marshal Massena's army opposite our lines, and very fairly said, 'But what could we do? If we did not find the provisions we must have starved ourselves; and you know soldiers will not do that, nor anyone else if he can possibly avoid it by any means.'

He was a good-natured man, and had great pity for the Portuguese nation, and looked upon the war as most abominable and unjust; and he often told me he was heartily tired of war and all its horrid attributes, but that it was not in his power to leave the army and return to France. He had asked leave, but was refused, and seemed very glad to have been taken prisoner, hoping that there might be some chance of getting home.

The pursuit of the enemy army continued and,. I think about the third day's march, coming suddenly upon a small party of them we made them prisoners. But, judge of our astonishment to find in the person of one of them an Irishman who was a lieutenant in one of our best regiments, and who had deserted a few weeks previously, and was, at the time he was missing from his regiment, supposed to have been made prisoner by some accident. I shall not mention the name of the regiment to which he belonged because he was a disgrace to it, and it was, and is, one of the best in the service. I shall merely say that he belonged to no regiment in the Light Division. He had been made *aide-de-camp* to the French general of division Loisson.

We very, soon delivered him up to the provost-marshal, to be taken to Lord Wellington, in hopes he would have had him shot upon the spot; but his lordship, having made inquiries about him from the officers of his regiment, was inclined to think the miserable man was not right in his senses, having formerly been insane. He therefore sent him a prisoner to England, with a recommendation that he might be permitted to resign his commission without any further inquiry about the matter, in order to spare his friends the pain of his conduct becoming public. This unfortunate man was not a person whose family was of any note or even known in the remotest way to Lord Wellington, so that his merciful and delicate conduct towards him was from pure good feeling and a reluctance to do a harsh thing when he could by any justifiable means avoid it.

One day on our march we found sixty or seventy poor donkeys who had been hamstrung by the French in a shamefully cruel manner, cutting the sinews of the hind-legs just above the hocks, and leaving the poor animals to die by inches. Now it might have been necessary to prevent the animals from falling into our hands, but why not have shot them at once, and not maim them in that cruel manner? The same day we passed by a village in a wild place where we found numbers of the inhabitants lying dead of starvation; among them were many little children, others just alive, and that was all; and those who were able going down on their knees supplicating a morsel of bread from our soldiers.

We were horror-struck at this heart-rending sight, and as the men were ordered to halt for a few minutes, with one consent they instantly collected from each other what little biscuit they had left, and which they knew was to last them as their only subsistence for two days longer, without the least chance of receiving any more as there was none up with the army; this they distributed to the miserable, starving survivors of this wretched hamlet. I doubt whether those good people who talk of the army as if soldiers were a set of unfeeling, hard-hearted, irreligious brutes, would have done as our soldiers did with truly genuine charity. It is an easy thing to talk about the necessity of charity, but a very different one to put it in execution when you know that by so doing you are depriving yourself of the means of existence, as the soldiers knew they were doing, and did, in consequence of this act of charity, go without food for two days and hard worked all the time, and many of them were left behind ill from weakness in consequence.

On arriving at the plain of Redinha which was of large extent, the river running between it and the village, the enemy drew up his forces in order of battle with the. river and village in his rear, the road to the village running over a long causeway and narrow bridge. He sent all his baggage to the other side of the village and waited during this operation for us to attack him; but as soon as all was clear the French Army commenced moving towards the bridge, leaving Marshal Ney with the rearguard of about twenty thousand men to keep us in check, which he did most skilfully and gallantly; and although Lord Wellington had nearly his whole force drawn up he did not think it prudent to do more than advance in line towards the enemy, and make a slight attack with the light troops and cavalry and Sir Lowry Cole's division. So Marshal Ney made good his retreat and took up his position in rear of the village of Redinha, his pickets occupying half the village and ours the other half.

It was my friend Captain Mein of the 52nd who commanded our picket; and when all was quiet and his sentinels posted and no fear of any surprise, he asked the captain commanding the enemy's pickets to have some supper with him, which the poor fellow, who had been half-starved for some months, was delighted to accept. So he came to

Mein's house, and after a good supper—for we had some sutlers come up to the army and an hour or two of conversation, it was time for him to go back to his own picket; and he had not been gone above a quarter of an hour when he was ordered to retreat from his post. Our men, perceiving that the French sentinels were withdrawn, gave the alarm and off started Mein with his picket after his friend the French captain, firing at him as hard as he could. You see by this that there is never any personal animosity between soldiers opposed to each other in war, but I daresay it strikes you as very odd that men should shake hands with each other, drink and eat together, laugh and joke, and then in a few minutes use every exertion of mind and body to destroy one another. But so it is, and I hope always will be the case. I should hate to fight out of personal malice or revenge, but have no objection to fight for '*fun and glory.*'

During the early part of this day I received a ball which went through my coat, waistcoat, and shirt, and hit me just over the heart, but only made a bruise and razed the skin. The bullet was fired at so great a distance that it was spent, and when I opened my waistcoat and shirt, expecting to find a hole in my body, the ball dropped quite flat, as if it had been struck by a hammer. This was a narrow escape. A little while afterwards I was standing talking to a friend, the adjutant of the regiment Mr. Winterbottom (now paymaster of the 52nd) with my hand resting on the pommel of his saddle, when a cannon shot passed between us and, as he poor fellow thought, only grazed his thigh; but when we came to examine it, the shot had done him more injury than he expected, and he was laid up in hospital with that wound six or seven months, and suffered a great deal of pain. He, Winterbottom, had risen from the rank of private soldier in my company, by his excellent and gallant conduct upon all occasions, and never for one instant did he fail in his duty.

One of the clearest-headed, coolest, and bravest men I ever saw in action, and the best adjutant in the army, either in the orderly room or the field; he has served through the whole of the Peninsular war, and was severely wounded several times; he was also badly wounded at Waterloo, and having been twice passed over when a company was vacant in the regiment after the peace, he was so mortified and disappointed, that he took the paymastership and went on half-pay as a lieutenant. I must tell you a trait of him which does honour to his head and heart. His parents were, as you may suppose, cottagers, and from the moment he enlisted and left them, he always sent them a part of his pay; and when the war was over, and he came home an officer with a sum of money which he had saved, having had some prize money, the first thing he did was to go and see his aged parents, build them a cottage and garden, and allow them a sufficient yearly sum of money to enable them to live comfortably and keep a servant girl to attend upon them.

Now this was most creditable and proper, for although it would have been very wrong had he not done so, few men would have perhaps acted so *judiciously* in placing his parents in their own rank of life, making them perfectly comfortable in every respect, but not having the foolish vanity, because he had become an officer, to put them in a situation above their old acquaintances and neighbours, where they would be considered as intruders and upstarts, instead of being happy, respected, and comfortable in the society they were used to and were brought up in. I think my friend Winterbottom is one of the best, most sensible, and honourable men I know, and I shall always feel a pride in his friendship as well as a satisfaction in having acted towards him when under my command in every way I thought most conducive to his welfare; and it will always be most gratifying to me to have it in my power to serve him, for he well deserves every possible assistance from any of the old hands of the 52nd who for so many years witnessed his upright and steady conduct.

A day or two after the affair of Redinha we had a hard day's work. About half an hour before daybreak our division was under arms, and while standing in close column, Sir William Erskine, who commanded us during General Craufurd's absence (who had gone to England on leave), came up and asked why we were not in march and following the enemy. Colonel Ross said because the enemy were *not* gone, but were within cannon shot of us at that very moment, for the captains of the pickets, Napier, 43rd, and Dobbs, 52nd, had patrolled up to their sentinels a short time before, and reported that the enemy was still in position. This did not satisfy Sir William Erskine, who kept blustering and swearing it was all nonsense and that the captains of the pickets knew nothing about the matter, and that there was not a man of them there.

Just as he spoke the fog, which had been very dense, cleared away a little, and bang came a shot from a twelve-pounder which struck the head of our column and made a lane through it killing and wounding many men; immediately a second and third, and then commenced a regular cannonade. Still the wise Sir William was sure it could be nothing but a single gun or two and a picket of the enemy and desired Colonel Ross to send my company to drive them in on the flank, at the same time sending an *aide-de-camp* to point out to me where I was to go to. We proceeded a short distance into some vine fields in a little bottom or valley upon the left flank of our column, the mist being very heavy, and just as we reached the bottom, *whiz* came a few shots from some of the enemy close to us but whom we saw not.

One of these shots went through my cap just grazing my forehead. I turned round to pick up my cap and to ask the *aide-de-camp* a question, when I saw him just putting spurs to his horse to gallop off back to his worthy general, as he thought it quite unnecessary to remain any longer! He was a young man just come out, and I dare say knew no better; but have no doubt he learned his duty before he was much older, or had the prudence to go home as I never saw or heard of the young gentleman afterwards. I pushed forward immediately, and had just leaped with the men over a low wall into a narrow road, and was almost instantly charged by a squadron of dragoons which was waiting for us behind some trees.

However, by this time it was broad daylight and the mist nearly dispersed; so perceiving what it was, and seeing the French officer commanding the squadron at its head, I had just time to form up half a dozen file and, giving the gentlemen a volley, down came the officer and a few of his men and horses, upon which the rest galloped off and I instantly made my company leap over the opposite wall into a vineyard where I knew I was safe from their cavalry; and forming a line of skirmishers, I advanced towards a French brigade which was drawn up at some distance in my front. However, they sent forward a cloud of sharpshooters to oppose me, and in a few minutes the action became very sharp.

I continued advancing, but very slowly, for they were quadruple my strength; which my commanding officer, who was following with the regiment, perceiving, sent several other companies to my support, and ere long we were four hundred strong, under Major Stewart, of the Rifle Corps. We then made a grand push, and drove the enemy from vineyard to vineyard, constantly advancing and keeping up a hot fire, the whole Light Division supporting us.

At this time poor Major Stewart received a shot through his body, several other officers were also wounded, and the command again devolved upon me. It was now about mid-day, and as my men had nearly expended all their ammunition, I was giving some directions to my lieutenant, Gifford—he was a few steps before me, and I had just turned round—when I saw some Frenchmen, who were concealed among the bushes, start up, and as poor Gifford's back was turned towards them while he was receiving orders from me, the muzzles of their muskets were within two or three yards of his head, when they fired, and he fell!

I rushed forward, caught him up in my arms, when to my horror his head fell back and his brains literally splashed on the ground! My excellent and valued friend was a corpse! The back of his skull was blown off! Some of my men who saw the whole thing at the same instant, dashing forward, plunged their bayonets into the Frenchmen's bodies and revenged the death of their officer. I laid his body gently on the ground; the soldiers wrapped it up in his cloak, and under a heavy fire from the enemy dug a grave in the sandy soil, and in this rough but glorious sepulchre were deposited the remains of Theophilus Gifford, as honourable, generous, gallant, and guileless a soldier as ever the fate of war cut off in the prime of youth, health, and spirits! The soldiers then fired a volley over his grave, which volley carried death to some brave fellows in the enemy's ranks, and thus in the space of a quarter of an hour finished the life and funeral of my friend! To this hour, when the circumstances of that melancholy day come to my recollection it affects me deeply, though it is now near twenty years since it happened. But such is la *fortune de la guerre*, and soldiers must make up their minds to submit to all these sorrowful occurrences in their profession.

As soon as I got my men supplied with fresh ammunition I moved forward with all the companies under my command, my brother William being my second as he was next senior officer. We drove the enemy from hill to hill with great slaughter, and about three o'clock, while leading on my men to charge a strong body of French which was a few yards before me, and which I thought I might be able to take prisoners, I received a shot in my right wrist which completely shattered it and forced me to go to the rear, as I was also very much fatigued, having been incessantly engaged with the enemy from three o'clock in the morning to past three o'clock in the day. To show that it was pretty hot work I need only mention that I went into action with sixty-six soldiers, three sergeants, and three subalterns, and I lost one officer, one sergeant, and ten or twelve soldiers killed; myself, two sergeants, and about fifteen or sixteen wounded, so that of my original number nearly half were killed and wounded.

As I went to the rear I saw some men carrying an officer in a blanket who seemed badly wounded, and when I came up to them I found it was my brother William, who had received a shot in the back while giving orders to his company. I and everyone who saw him thought it was a mortal wound, but it proved otherwise, thank God! although from the circumstance of his never being able to get the ball extracted, he often suffers considerable pain from it. [2]

We were obliged to lie down under the shade of a tree at the roadside waiting till the columns had passed, as the rest of the army was marching to the support of the Light Division. While waiting under this tree, who should come up but our brother Charles, who was with his regiment, having joined from Lisbon that morning although his wound in the face was not quite healed. He was sorry to find us both wounded so severely, and was himself suffering from weakness and want of food, as he had not been able to get anything to eat for the last two days and had been continually on horseback pushing on to join the army, being one of those who never remained behind when the troops were advancing unless forced to do so by wounds and sickness, and not even then unless in so weak a state as to preclude his sitting on his horse.

While waiting with us under the tree, one of his own officers came up and said, 'Major, here is our surgeon, who is very clever at *taking off an extremity*; if you like him to try his hand on your brother's arm he will do it elegantly,' upon which Charles swore that if the little doctor came near me he would shoot him! I laughed immoderately at Charles' rage and assured him he need not be afraid for I would not let anyone take it off; but, as you see, it was destined to go at a future period!

As soon as the road was pretty well clear we bid Charles goodbye and proceeded to the town of Condexa, William carried in his blanket and I walking alongside of him. On our road we were joined by several other officers, all wounded, and ten or a dozen of us went into the only house we could find habitable, as the enemy the moment they left a town set fire to it in all directions to prevent us as they said from finding any shelter. The consequence was that ruin and desolation spread throughout Portugal! I can never agree to the doctrine that the French were justified by the rules of war in so doing, because the professed object could not be gained by it, as means would always be found of securing to us, the advancing army and allies of the in-

---

2. And did so all his life.—Ed. (W.N.)

habitants, everything that was necessary. How different was Sir John Moore's conduct in his retreat! His constant endeavour was to prevent the slightest destruction of the property of the inhabitants; and when urged by many of his generals and friends to destroy the bridges, he replied, 'No; why ruin and distress the unfortunate people more than absolute necessity demands for our own safety?'

But the truth is that Marshal Massena was so enraged at being baffled by Lord Wellington, and forced to retreat from Portugal and losing Lisbon which he thought was in his grasp, that he vented his rage and disappointment in wanton acts of destruction and oppression against the wretched inhabitants of Portugal. A French colonel who was made prisoner that day and was in the house with me told me that he had the execution of orders to burn every town and village they passed, and boasted of the regular and expeditious manner in which he performed it, placing all the furniture in the houses in the rooms below and then setting fire to it by soldiers who were placed in each house with firebrands, and all by sound of bugle so that every house was in a blaze at the same moment.

When we got a little settled upstairs we were all examined by the surgeons, and on probing William's wound they told me they feared it might prove mortal; mine they said would be very tedious and most probably I should lose the use of several of my fingers. Poor Major Stewart died that night holding my hand; and he blamed an officer high in rank as the cause of his death, this person having said something to him in the execution of his duty which made Stewart gallop forward, when he was immediately shot by the enemy. The conduct of that officer was quite unwarrantable, but as he is also gone I shall not mention his name, but merely say he never had the character of a *brave* man while in our division, notwithstanding he said that which caused the death of as fine, enterprising, and gallant a soldier as ever faced the enemy. Had poor Stewart lived he would have distinguished himself highly; as it was, he held a high place in the estimation of his brother officers and Lord Wellington.

Lord March came to see us that night, and to say that Lord Wellington had written to my mother to inform her of our being wounded, and that he was well satisfied with our conduct on that day. This was most kind and considerate of him, who was commander-in-chief of the army and had scarcely time to eat! His time and thoughts were fully occupied, yet he found a moment to do a kind act which he knew would highly gratify my mother and ease her mind about her sons' wounds. Lord March also showed us every kindness possible; he had ridden that evening twenty miles to see us, and returned to headquarters after a few hours' stay with us. But he was always the kindest of friends, and I have never found the least difference in his friendship of now two-or three-and-twenty years.

This same night another officer came to see us with whom at that time we were totally unacquainted. This officer was marching with his regiment, the 4th Dragoons, through the town and hearing there were several wounded officers in a house without much to eat or drink, he came up to us and said he had brought all the provisions he had with him and requested our acceptance of them; and he would not hear of our leaving him a morsel for himself, and wishing us a speedy cure, he went after his regiment leaving bread, wine, tea and sugar, &c. This officer's name was Light. Of course this was a kindness never to be forgotten, and we have ever since been on terms of great intimacy with him.

It is a great pity he quitted the army, as he had highly distinguished himself and was a great favourite with Lord Wellington, who had promoted him for his conduct. He is a very clever fellow, and from his knowledge of languages and drawing, &c., &c., he soon brought himself into notice. Thus you see, boys, how necessary it is to be good linguists as well as to be well acquainted with military drawing and geography; particularly to you who must depend upon your own exertions in your profession for preferment, as you know I can do no more than give you a good education and then the rest must depend upon your own good conduct and activity.'

Having given you an instance of the kindness of an officer, I shall give you one of a private soldier of my own company, which gratified me more than anything at the time. My servant came and told me that John Dunn, an Irishman whom I had enlisted several years before, wished to see me. When he came into the room he immediately said:

'Och, captain, but I'm come to see how you and your brother is after the wounds. Didn't I see you knocked over by the bloody Frenchmen's shot? and sure I thought you was kilt. But myself knew you wouldn't be plaised if I didn't folly on after the villains, so I was afeard to go pick you up when ye was kilt, long life to you! But I pursued the inimy as long as I was able, and sure I couldn't do more; and now I'm come to see your honour, long life to you agin.'

I shook hands with him and said, 'But, John, you seem wounded

---

1. This chapter is composed of unfinished notes from Mrs. Gamewell's pen.

yourself; why is your arm tied up?'

'Och, nothing at all to prevent me coming to see your honour, and your honour's brother lying there, Captain William, long life to him! I hope he's not dead.' Upon insisting to know if he was wounded, at last he replied, 'Why sure it's nothing, only me *arrum* was cut off a few hours ago below the elbow joint, and I couldn't come till the anguish was over a bit. But now I'm here, and thank God your honour's arrum is not cut off, for it's mighty cruel work; by Jasus, I'd rather be shot twenty times, though the doctor tould me he did it asy too, long life to his honour! I'm sure he didn't mean to hurt me all he could help.'

I then asked him for his brother, who was also a recruit of mine and in the company, and an uncommonly fine, handsome soldier as ever stepped, and who was a particular favourite of mine. He hesitated a few moments, and heaving a convulsive sob said; 'I seed him shot through the heart alongside wid me just as I got the shot myself, and he looked up piteously in my face and said, "Oh, John dear, my poor mother!" And sure I couldn't look at him again for the life of me, my heart was broke, and I came away to the rare. But, captain, he died like a soldier, as your honour would wish him to die, and sure that's enough. He had your favour whilst he lived, God be with him, he's gone now.'

After this anecdote who will dare to say private soldiers have no feelings? By Heavens! it makes my anger rise and my blood boil to hear people talk of soldiers as if they were a different race of beings from themselves. Here was a poor fellow, an Irishman and a Catholic, who, out of pure affection for his officer, having seen his brother killed by his side in action, and suffered the amputation of his own arm, walks near seven miles, without meat or drink, to see his captain, who he knew was severely wounded! Could a brother have done more? Brave comrade, I never can, or ever will, forget your conduct on that day. As long as I have the means you shall not want if I am aware of it. He was sent home and well pensioned, and has ever since been travelling about England as a hawker or pedlar.

I have several times well clothed him, fed him, and started him afresh with a new set of little things to sell, and twice taken him out of gaol, to which he had been sent for not having a regular licence to sell; indeed, for two or three years after the war he was an expensive job! I think he cost me about fifteen or twenty pounds a year; but latterly I was obliged to be more strict with him, and fairly tell him I could only give him relief once a year, because I got him a large pension and he had nothing to provide. But I am afraid I must confess my old comrade has the failing, so habitual to old discharged soldiers, of not being able to refrain from drink whenever it can be had; something like my other poor old soldier, Mark Cann, whom you know so well, and who will soon kill himself I am afraid; but till he does cease to exist I must be kind to him. The last time I saw Dunn he promised me faithfully he would 'take up' and give over drinking; and as I have not seen him for two or three years, I am in hopes he is doing well, being perfectly certain that whenever he is in any distress he will make his appearance at my house; indeed, he has directions for so doing. He married a woman with some money and respectable relations, but they parted in consequence of 'the drop of drink,' as he told me himself; and added, with an arch expression of his eye, 'and no blame till her.'

And now, boys, whenever you see a poor lame soldier, recollect John Dunn, and never, as you value my love and affection, pass him coldly by. You never saw a soldier sent from my door without inquiry into his case; and never shall, if I know it, for I conceive it to be my bounden duty to see and relieve those who, although from circumstances in a lower grade than myself, fought as bravely and bled as freely as I ever did for that country which is the common parent of all Britons! and for whose cause the private soldier fights with as much enthusiasm as the general; and without the soldier's—I mean the private soldier's—steady, intrepid, and gallant execution of his duty, where would be the military glory that has saved England? Mind, in the word military I include naval service and naval heroes. I look upon them as the same.

In a few days William's wound took a favourable turn, and we all proceeded in a waggon to the city of Coimbra, where by this time the hospitals were established; and as it was not exactly in the line of retreat the French took all the houses were untouched and the inhabitants were daily returning to it, so that before we got there many houses were occupied, and all the colleges and monasteries filled rapidly with students and priests. Here we were treated kindly and had as much comfort as we could wish or expect, and were skilfully and feelingly attended to by our own medical officers, who were indefatigable in their endeavours to make every officer and soldier under their care as comfortable as they could.

And I must say that the whole of the civil department of the army at Coimbra was excellent in every particular, as well as active in the zealous discharge of their respective duties. I am anxious to state this, because I have seen the very contrary conduct at other times.

A few days after we were settled at Coimbra our brother Charles got leave to come and see how we were getting on. He found William walking about, convalescent; but my wound, from the bone being so shattered, had taken a bad turn and I suffered very much. We gave him plenty to eat and drink, which was a great treat to him poor fellow for he had been on short allowance ever since we parted. The next day he was obliged to be off, and having seen us and his mind being relieved he joined his regiment in much better health and spirits.

Coimbra was at this time made a depot for the army, and an officer appointed commandant, whose duty it was to look after all the hospitals, the sick and wounded, as well as all the civil departments; to see that all recruits and reinforcements for the army were properly kept in order and equipped, ready to march at a moment's warning to join their respective corps, &c.; and as often as a body of men were dismissed from hospital as fit for duty, he appointed such officers as were also recovered to command them and march with them to the army. It is a very troublesome and arduous duty that of commandant, and a difficult thing to find a good one, because the best officers do not like to accept it (though double pay) as it keeps them in the rear and out of action; but it is of essential consequence to have a good one and quite impossible to do without them.

About a month after we had been at Coimbra, William, being sufficiently recovered though his wound was not healed, joined the division and was appointed brigade major to the second brigade, under Colonel Beckwith (now a general and K.C.B.), who is one of the best general officers in the field that I know of. He is never at a loss, always cool, and particularly skilful at penetrating the intentions of the enemy, and always ready to oppose him in the very nick of time; and as to his gallantry, no man was more conspicuous for intrepid conduct. William has a high opinion of his abilities as an officer and has mentioned him highly in his history of the Peninsular War.

About three weeks after William left me, I had been sitting up late in a room adjoining my bedroom and trying to write with my left hand and to mend pens, but being fatigued, I left the lamp burning, and my penknife on the table and went to bed, hanging up my watch and sword over my pillow. About an hour or two afterwards I awoke, thinking I heard a noise in the room, and listening attentively I heard something which I supposed was a rat; but as the lamp was gone out in the other room and it was quite dark, I could not distinguish anything.

In a few minutes I distinctly heard a noise as if my clothes were being dragged about. I then was certain someone was in the room and stealing my things, so I got up softly and taking down my sword, which was in a steel scabbard, I went gently to the door, listened very attentively, but could hear no sound and was on the point of returning to bed, when I thought I would just cross the other room and try if the passage door was open. In doing this I suddenly came in contact with a man, who instantly seized me round the waist and made, every effort to throw me down. Thinking he was a Portuguese I expected every moment to have a stiletto plunged into my body, well knowing that a Portuguese thief would not come unprepared for assassination in case of discovery.

I struggled hard with the fellow, and recollecting that I had left one of the windows open which was very high from the ground I attempted, as well as I was able, with only one hand (the other being bound up and the bones not knit together again) to get him with his back against it, so that I could then throw him out into the street, which would have settled him forever. But in this, from weakness, I failed. I then made an effort to approach the table, where I had left the penknife open, with which I might stab him before he stabbed me; but I had not strength to push him along; and finding that he had not made any attempt to kill me, I began to suspect that he must be an English soldier, and therefore struck at him with the hilt of my sword in the face, and calling to him said that if he would speak I would let him go.

But speak he would not, and suddenly, as if recollecting himself, he seized my wounded arm in his teeth, and gave me such pain by tearing at it, that I let go my sword, and being exhausted by so long a struggle, I had no more power, and the fellow immediately picked it up, drew it out of the scabbard, and began cutting at me as well as he could in the dark. However, I got under the table, and by that means avoided his blows. Finding he could do nothing more and that by this time a medical officer, who lodged opposite me, was up and alarmed by my calling out for assistance, he cut open a glass door with my sword, which opened into a balcony and from thence let himself down into the street and got off just as my servant came into the room, who immediately ran to the window and levelled his musket at him, but it missed fire and my friend escaped.

As soon as we got a light, we found he had removed my trunk and all my clothes into the passage and had everything piled up ready to carry off. When I went to my bed I found the rascal had taken my gold watch, which I was very much vexed at, as it was an old family one, given me by poor William Craig before he died. I never could trace this robbery, or get the least clue to the perpetrator of it; and, indeed, I was very glad of it, for had I found him out he would have been hanged, and as he certainly had no intention of doing me any bodily harm when he first entered my room I should never have felt comfortable if he had been hung. The struggling and the laceration of the wound by his teeth, in my weak state, brought on fever and I was laid up in bed for some weeks after and my recovery much retarded, and I was prevented joining my regiment as soon as I had hoped to have done.

CHAPTER 5

Siege of Ciudad Rodrigo

Before I left Coimbra I received a letter from Lord Wellington's military secretary, to inform me that his lordship had recommended me as well as my brother William for the brevet rank of major in the army, in consequence of our conduct, and particularly on the day we were last wounded. This was a pleasing communication, as I had been a captain eight years and began to fear I never should be promoted, although I never was a moment absent from my duty except when disabled by wounds. When I joined the army the Light Division was on the march towards the south. I wished at that period very much to be allowed to enter the Portuguese service as a lieutenant-colonel commanding a regiment, and therefore I asked Lord Wellington's permission to make application to Marshal Beresford to appoint me to the command of a Light Infantry regiment, as the Portuguese army was under the command of the marshal.

Lord Wellington granted my request and accordingly I went to Marshal Beresford, who received me very kindly, said he would appoint me with pleasure to a Light Infantry regiment which happened to be vacant at that very time. I was delighted at this and went off to get my things ready, &c., but I found that our general (Craufurd), having heard of my application to enter the Portuguese army, had gone to Lord Wellington and represented that he had been at great pains to make good field officers in the Light Division, and that if he was to be deprived of them in this way the division would be ruined; and as he was pleased to say I was one of his best officers he positively refused to let me go out of his division. He would have been content if the marshal would appoint me to one of the Portuguese light regiments in his own division which was commanded by a Portuguese colonel whom Craufurd did not like; but this was out of the question, and

Lord Wellington therefore acquiesced in General Craufurd's demand that I should remain where I was. This was very annoying to me, but from the flattering manner General Craufurd had spoken of me to the commander-in-chief, I could not be angry; and indeed I think he was right not to permit those officers who had been constantly serving with him and formed under his own directions in the finest division in the army, to be taken from him just as their long experience had made them more valuable to him.

Lord Wellington sent for me the next day and told me he was very sorry for my disappointment but that he hoped it would be made up to me by his informing me I was made major of the 52nd Regiment, and although I actually belonged to the second battalion, which was in England, I should remain on service with the first battalion. This put me in such good spirits that I cared very little about going into the Portuguese service. I went, however, to inform Marshal Beresford and to thank him for his kindness. He was not very well pleased with General Craufurd and expressed himself in pretty strong terms on the occasion. And I am not surprised at it, because he was very anxious to get officers of some experience into the Portuguese army, which, whatever may be Lord Beresford's abilities in other respects, was certainly indebted to his conduct and unwearied care, attention, and skilful management for the high state of discipline and good conduct it attained and preserved during the whole war; and certainly no troops were more conspicuous for gallantry and orderly conduct.

In my humble opinion this was owing to Marshal Beresford's own personal exertions, and he is fully entitled to the praise he has received from all persons competent to judge in that respect. When he took the command of the Portuguese Army it was sunk into the lowest state of degradation, disorder, meanness, and bigotry; neither honour, honesty, nor bravery was to be found in it. Many officers were holding civil situations incompatible with the performance of their military duties; others, I believe, were actually servants in great families; and every regiment had its patron saint, who was generally a captain and sometimes a major, and his pay went to pamper the appetites and debaucheries of the monks of his convent.

About this time my friend General Ross, then lieutenant-colonel commanding the 52nd Regiment (poor Colonel Barclay having died of his wounds), was about to leave the regiment and go home. He sent for me one morning and told me he wished I would go to General Hill's corps and see my friend Colonel Colborne, who commanded the 66th Regiment, and tell him that he would exchange regiments with him if he liked, as he thought by so doing he would do the greatest service to the 52nd, as he well knew the high opinion Sir John Moore had of him and that his great abilities and character pointed him out as the best person to be in command of the regiment.

Ross being determined to leave the regiment and go home, I was delighted that he had himself fixed upon the officer most proper to succeed him, and who was my greatest friend next to himself; but I never saw anyone suffer more poignancy of real grief than Ross did on leaving a regiment he had served in since he was a boy, and had highly distinguished himself as commanding officer, and every officer and soldier of which would have willingly laid down their life for him and followed him anywhere he chose to lead them, so much was he looked up to, honoured, and respected both for his own character and as the favourite of Sir John Moore. The morning of the day Ross left us he divided his watch, chain, and seals among his greatest friends. The watch, which is the gold one I wear, he gave to me, and it has ever since been my constant companion and will be to the hour of my death. It had belonged also to poor Captain Powis (a brother of Lord Lilford), who was killed at Badajos.

Colonel Colborne soon joined us; and taking the command of the 52nd, it fought under his superintendence many a battle, stormed many a town, and distinguished itself by its perfect discipline and steady, cool intrepidity as much as any regiment ever yet did in any army in the world, thus proving that the system of discipline acquired under Sir John Moore and Colonel Kenneth Mackenzie had infused such zeal and spirit into both officers and soldiers that few regiments equalled, and none ever surpassed, it! I look back with pride and delight to the many happy years I passed in that beloved corps, where every officer was a high-minded gentleman and every private a gallant and well-conducted soldier. In it I passed the most active period of my military life, and rose from junior lieutenant to lieutenant-colonel; and all the professional fame I may have acquired I feel is due to the conduct of the gallant and excellent soldiers I had the honour to command.

In every action I was ever in I knew I had but to lead, and that I should be ably backed and well followed up; no necessity to *look behind* when at the head of 52nd Light Infantry men! Every officer in it I was proud to call my comrade; and all those who have survived the war are now among my dearest and warmest friends, but I grieve to say they are but few. By the blessing of God and the kindness of the commander-in-chief, I hope to see my dear son George enter the army as an ensign in that regiment; and, perhaps, many years hence, if I ever become a general I may be colonel of it myself, and then I think I shall wish for nothing more! But I fear there never will be any chance of that. Indeed, when I consider that Sir John Colborne is only a few years older than myself I cannot wish it, as the moment the 52nd Regiment is vacant he will get it, for they could not possibly give it to any other man after the distinguished and brilliant services he has performed at the head of it.

We were continually moving about till January 8, 1812, when we broke ground before the fortress of Ciudad Rodrigo, one of the frontier towns on the north of Portugal, and from which we had retreated to the lines about a year and a half before. There was a small fort outside the works of the town, with a small party to defend it. Two companies of each of the regiments of the Light Division were ordered to attack it as soon as it was night. I volunteered to command this party, but Lord Wellington said whoever was the first field officer for duty should command, and as Colonel Colborne was the first, he got it. The colonel formed his party, and gave his orders so explicitly, and so clearly made every officer understand what he was to do, that no mistake could possibly be made.

The consequence was that in twenty minutes from the time he moved to the attack the fort was stormed and carried. The watchword of 'England and St. George' was heard shouted loud and strong, and re-echoed by the division, which was under arms, and in a few moments came a report from Colonel Colborne that every man in the fort was either killed, wounded, or prisoner. We lost a few men and some officers wounded, among whom was my friend Captain Mein, who was shot through the thigh, and was sent to the rear to hospital, and recovered soon enough to be at the siege of Badajos, where he was again wounded in the assault—shot through the other thigh.

After the fort was taken we immediately pushed forward some sharpshooters to keep up a fire and mislead the enemy, while the Engineers commenced marking out the parallels, &c. The ground being soft, the great thing was to work hard with the spade, and very soon the trenches were began. Each division took twenty-four hours in the trenches, and upon being relieved the next day marched back to its cantonments. Our division had a river to pass, both going to and returning from the trenches, and as it was very frosty weather, and sometimes sleet and snow, we found it terribly cold going through the water above our knees and sometimes up to the waist; and when going for the twenty-four hours of duty in the trenches it was hard work, for we were not allowed any fire all night, the men and officers cooking their provisions before they went, so that our clothes used to freeze on us, and we became so stiff and cold that we were forced to drink lots of brandy to keep us warm inside at all events.

About three weeks before the assault of the town I was field officer of the trenches, and was standing with some men who were digging a trench, when a thirteen-inch shell from the town fell in the midst of us. I called to the men to lie down flat on the ground, as by that means most probably few, if any, would receive injury. The men, knowing this, instantly obeyed orders and lay flat, except one of them, an Irishman, and an old marine, but a most worthless, drunken dog, who ran up to the shell, the fuze of which was still burning, and striking it a blow with his spade knocked it out, and taking the immense shell in his hands came and presented it to me, saying, 'There she is for you now, your honour. By Jasus, she'll do you no harm, since I knocked the life out of the cratur.' I never saw a cooler thing, and of course was *obliged* to give him a dollar and leave to get drunk if he got safe home to the cantonments. He told me he had often done the same thing in Egypt, where he had served under Abercrombie.

The same night I was standing talking to Colborne near a battery which we were finishing, when *bounce* came a shell among us, and before we had time to lie down burst with a proper crack, killed two poor fellows, wounded several, one of whom had both legs taken off close to the hip. I received a severe bruise and scrape, but, although I was knocked down by it, no further injury. It struck me on the top of the shoulder, but luckily it was the top of the shell which fell on me after having been blown up into the air and lost its force. The next day, as I thought from all I saw and heard from the engineers that ere long the breaches would be practicable, I went to General Craufurd and asked him as a favour that he would allow me to command the storming party of the Light Division whenever the commander-in-chief determined on making the assault.

This he promised, and on January 19, 1812, we received orders to move from our cantonments and march to the trenches. About a mile from the town we halted, and General Craufurd desired me to get one hundred volunteers from each British regiment in the division, with proportionate officers and non-commissioned officers, to form them up in front of the division, and take the command of them in order to lead the assault. I went to three regiments—*viz.*, the 43rd, 52nd, and Rifle Corps, and said, 'Soldiers, I have the honour to be appointed to the command of the storming party which is to lead the Light Division to the assault of the small breach. I want one hundred volunteers from each regiment; those who will go with me come forward.'

Instantly there rushed out nearly half the division, and we were obliged to take them at chance. I then formed them in companies of one hundred men each, Captain Fergusson commanding the 43rd, Captain Jones the 52nd (this officer afterwards volunteered to be of the storming party at Badajos, and was killed after behaving most gloriously; he received fifteen balls through his body!), Captain Mitchel commanded the Rifles. These were preceded by what is called the *forlorn hope* consisting of twenty-five men, two sergeants, and one subaltern, a lieutenant, because if he survives he gets a company. The officer who commanded in this instance was a great friend of mine, a very excellent gallant officer, Lieutenant Gurwood,[1] of the 52nd.

As soon as all was formed, we marched at the head of the division in high spirits, and determined that nothing should stop us from carrying the breach. I felt that I was on the point of fulfilling my old motto, '*Death or glory.*' I knew if I failed it must be my own fault, as I had at my back three hundred British bayonets, wielded by as able hands and stout ' hearts of oak ' as ever faced the enemy! that I had only to lead, to give the word, and all would be carried by British steel, let the opposition be ever so great. If I fell, I should fall as I wished; if I lived, most probably promotion, certainly glory, the soldier's greatest prize, would be my reward; and, above all, I knew I should receive the approbation of the commander of the army, Lord Wellington.

When it was nearly dark in the evening, the Light Division was formed behind the old convent on the outside of the town, nearly opposite the small breach. While waiting here for orders, I told a friend of mine, the assistant surgeon of the 52nd, Mr. Walker, that I had an idea I should lose my arm, and, if so, I hoped he would perform the operation of taking it off. A few minutes after Lord Wellington sent for Colonel Colborne and myself, and pointing out, as well as the light would permit, the spot where the foot of the breach was, he said to me, 'Now do you understand the way you are to lead, so as to arrive at the breach without noise or confusion?'

I answered, and we then went back to the regiment; and just before I moved on, some staff officer present said, 'Why, your men are not

---

1. Editor of the *Wellington Despatches*.—Ed.(W.N.)

loaded; why do you not make them load?'

I replied, 'Because if we do not do the business with the bayonet, without firing, we shall not be able to do it at all, so I shall not load.'

I heard Lord Wellington, who was close by, say, 'Let him alone; let him go his own way.'

The 3rd Portuguese Regiment of Caçadores, under Colonel Elder, was to carry bags filled with long dry grass, in order, by throwing them into the ditch, to prevent any accident as we leaped down into it, as it was deep, and thus prevent the jump from being so great. The signal of attack of both breaches—(there was a large breach at another part of the fortress attacked by the 3rd division, under General Picton)—being made, and the 3rd Caçadores not having arrived with the bags of grass (owing to some want of proper orders, as neither Colonel Elder nor his excellent regiment were likely to neglect any duty; and I am sure the blame rested else-where, for George Elder was always ready for any service; no man has distinguished himself more), I gave the order to move forward, cautioning the officers and men to be silent, and once having gained the breach, to wheel right and left, and clear the parapet on each side, in order to effect which without confusion my party was in double column of sections, the 43rd on the right, the 52nd on the left, Lieutenant Gurwood in advance a few yards with the forlorn hope.

We soon came to the ditch, and immediately jumping in, we rushed forward to the *fausse braie*, and having clambered up we proceeded towards the breach. But Lieutenant Gurwood and party, having, owing to the darkness of the night, gone too much to the left, was employed in placing ladders on the unbreached face of the bastion, when he got a shot in the head; but immediately recovering his feet he came up to me, and at that moment the engineer, or Captain Staveley of the staff corps, I cannot recollect which, called out, 'You are wrong; this way to the right is the breach;' and Captain Ferguson, myself, Gurwood, and the rest of the officers, and such men as were nearest the engineer officer, rushed on, and we all mounted the breach together, the enemy pouring a heavy fire on us.

When about two-thirds up, I received a grape shot which smashed my elbow and great part of my arm; and on falling, the men, who thought I was killed, checked for a few moments, and forgetting they were not loaded commenced snapping their muskets. I immediately called out 'Recollect you are not loaded; push on with the bayonet.' Upon this the whole gave a loud 'hurrah,' and driving all before them, carried the breach, and wheeling as I had given orders to the right and left soon drove off the enemy; and a part of the stormers under Captain Ferguson rushed down upon the enemy where they were defending the large breach, and commencing a flank fire upon them, soon drove them from their defences, and thus opened the way for the 3rd division to enter the town. Lieutenant Gurwood, who had pushed into the town, followed the garrison to the citadel, where the Governor surrendered, and delivering his sword to Gurwood the latter made him prisoner and took him to Lord Wellington, who immediately desired Lieutenant Gurwood to keep the governor's sword as a mark of his approbation.

During all this time the troops of the Light Division kept pouring into the place through the breach, and I kept cheering them on as well as I could, but I got terribly bruised and trampled upon in the confusion and darkness. However, very soon 'Victory! England forever!' was shouted by thousands, and then I knew all was right, and I waited patiently in the breach till all had passed, when I heard my name called several times, and upon answering, the Prince of Orange, Lord March, and Lord Fitzroy Somerset came up to me, and the prince taking off his sash (which I have) they tied up my arm, and with the help of a sergeant and some men I got down and proceeded to the old ruined convent, where I found numbers wounded and the surgeon very busy with his knife.

I learned here that General Craufurd was mortally wounded, and I saw General Vandeleur, who commanded our brigade, sitting on a stone waiting to be dressed, having been wounded in the shoulder. He is a fine, honourable, kind-hearted, gallant soldier, and an excellent man. I never knew him say or do a harsh thing to any human being. No man can or ought to be more respected than he is.

It soon came to my turn to have my arm amputated, and I then reminded my friend Walker, who was there, of his promise to me a few hours before, and begged he would be so good as to perform the operation; but he told me he could not, as there was a staff surgeon present, whose rank being higher, it was necessary he should do it, so Staff Surgeon Guthrie cut it off. However, for want of light, and from the number of amputations he had already performed, and other circumstances, his instruments were blunted, so it was a long time before the thing was finished, at least twenty minutes, and the pain was great. I then thanked him for his kindness, having sworn at him like a trooper while he was at it, to his great amusement, and I proceeded to find some place to lie down and rest, and after wandering and stumbling about the suburbs for upwards of an hour, I saw a light in a house, and on entering I found it full of soldiers, and a good fire blazing in the kitchen.

As I went towards the fire I saw a figure wrapped up in a cloak sitting in the corner of the chimney place apparently in great pain. Upon nearer inspection I found this was my friend John Colborne, who had received a severe wound in the shoulder. Upon asking me if I was wounded, I showed him the stump of my arm, which so affected him, poor fellow, that he burst into tears. He was in such horrid pain, his spirits were quite sunk, and he could not stand the sight of my loss. How often afterwards did he wish *his* arm had been taken off, for the sufferings he went through for two years afterwards were very great. His arm was broken close up to the joint of the shoulder, which, and the scapula itself, were split. The ball remained in the joint for two years, when at last it was taken out, and then he recovered, but has a stiff joint.

Never did any man suffer more patiently than he did. But it was *Colborne*, and that is sufficient, there being no suffering in human life which he would not endure, if necessary, either for his country or his friends. Few men are like him; indeed, except the Duke of Wellington, I know no officer in the British Army his equal. His expansive mind is capable of grasping anything, however difficult or abstruse; his genius in war so powerful that it overcomes all obstacles; and his splendid talents and long experience have gained him the admiration and confidence of the whole army, which looks up to Sir John Colborne, should a war take place, as the man who will rise conspicuous above all others.

The Duke of Wellington, from the time Colborne was a lieutenant-colonel, always placed the most entire confidence in him, and although only a lieutenant-colonel, employed him constantly in every enterprise of difficulty and danger, and never did he fail once. He has, with the most intrepid bravery, a coolness of head in the very heat of action which never fails him, and thus he penetrates with eagle eye into the enemy's intentions, and is sure to baffle his designs when least expected. Nothing can take him by surprise or flurry him; and I am confident, if Colborne was suddenly awoke out of his sleep and told he was surrounded by an army treble his numbers, it would only have the effect of making him, if possible, still more calm and collected, and that if it was possible for mortal man to get out of the scrape, he would.

His talents for civil government are also very great, as he has proved in Guernsey; and the Duke of Wellington and Sir George Murray have, in consequence of their high opinion of his abilities, sent him as governor to Upper Canada, where he is doing everything that marks the steady, upright, fearless, and able servant of his king and country, and where, if any dispute should unfortunately arise between England and America, his military skill will be of most essential service.

I cannot leave the subject of Ciudad Rodrigo without mentioning the death of one of my greatest friends and companions, Captain Joseph Dobbs, who was killed upon the ramparts. Never fell a braver soldier in the flower of youth, beloved and regretted by all who knew him. He was open, generous, and warm-hearted, enthusiastic in his profession, and just sufficiently romantic to make him enter into any project with spirit and ardour. An Irishman, like them he was gay and cheerful, with a spirit of honour marked by the most scrupulous integrity.

When his purse was full, it was open to all, and shared with his comrades; when empty, he only regretted it because he was thus deprived of the power of giving to all round him; but *being empty*, his high and independent spirit would make him submit to any personal deprivation rather than be under pecuniary obligations to any man. Such was my lamented friend Joe Dobbs. Arduous in his professional duties, honourable in his dealings with all men, generous, kind, and cheerful with his comrades, high spirited and daring, he met a soldier's glorious death while in the act of cheering his men to victory.

As soon as I could get a bed I went into it, but sleep was impossible, for the pain increased, and the inflammation got so high that in a couple of hours I was quite delirious, and remained so for the next twenty-four hours, after which I fell asleep and began gradually to get better. In the room above me was General Craufurd, dying from a wound, the shot having passed through his arm, entered his chest, and lodged in his lungs. He suffered dreadfully, his moans were very distressing to me, and more particularly so in consequence of his daily, nay, I may almost say, hourly, sending down messages to me to know how I was, and to express his approval of my conduct, and his regret that he should never see me again. I never shall forget this; I should be, what I am not, an unfeeling brute if I did!

Indeed, General Craufurd was always kind to me, and ready to do me a service when in his power. In a day or two he breathed his last, and thus a period was put to his long, faithful, and, I may add, brilliant services in many instances, for although he was a most unpopular man, every officer in the Light Division must acknowledge that by his unwearied and active exertions of mind and body that division was brought to a state of discipline and knowledge of the duties of light troops which never was equalled by any division in the British Army, or surpassed by any division of the French Army.

I do not mean, or wish to insinuate, that we were better than the others either in physical power or courage (all Englishmen are alike), but most unquestionably we understood our business better, and had a better system of marching and discipline than any other division, the proof of which is the use the Duke of Wellington made of us during the war. In every siege, in every battle, his despatches will bear me out in my estimation of the services and activity of the Light Division. Again: look at the extraordinary number of privates from our three regiments who were made officers, and who, the moment they joined their new regiments, were, almost without exception. made adjutants; and the number of field officers and commanding officers promoted from the 43rd, 52nd, and Rifle Corps proves the estimation in which His Royal Highness the Duke of York held the division under General Craufurd's command; and at the end of the Peninsular war nearly all the captains of those three regiments were majors by brevet, having received the rank for their services on the field of battle.

To give a sketch of General Craufurd's character is neither an easy nor a pleasant task, as truth compels me to acknowledge he had many and grave faults. Brilliant as some of the traits of his character were, and notwithstanding the good and generous feelings which often burst forth like a bright gleam of sunshine from behind a dark and heavy cloud, still there was a sullenness which seemed to brood in his inmost soul and generate passions which knew no bounds. As a general commanding a division of light troops of all arms, Craufurd certainly excelled. His knowledge of outpost duty was never exceeded by any British general, and I much doubt if there are many in any other service who know more of that particular branch of the profession than he did. He had, by long experience, unwearied zeal, and constant activity, united to practice, founded a system of discipline and marching which arrived at such perfection that he could calculate to the minute the time his whole division, baggage, commissariat, &c., &c., would take to arrive at any given point, no matter how many days' march.

Every officer and soldier knew his duty in every particular, and also knew he must perform it. No excuse would save him from the general's rage if he failed in a single iota. As a commissary he was perfect, and if provisions were to be got within his possible reach his division never was without them. His mental activity was only surpassed by his physical powers. The moment his division arrived at its ground for the night he never moved from his horse till he had made himself master of every part of his post, formed his plan for its defence if necessary, and explained all his arrangements to the staff officers and the field officers of each regiment, so that if his orders were strictly obeyed a surprise was impossible.

He was seldom deceived in the strength of the enemy's outposts, for he reconnoitred them with the eye of one who knew his business well; and although in some few instances he got into scrapes, it was more through vanity than anything else, as he was so vain of the division he commanded, that he really had persuaded himself he might oppose it to any number of the enemy; and when once in action he was obstinately bent upon holding his ground at any risk, and in the heat of the battle often let his temper get the better of his judgement.

The action with Marshal Ney's corps at the Coa was a proof of this. I am inclined to think that, had he lived, he would have altered his conduct in many particulars, and conquered in some measure the extraordinary bursts of passion which knew no bounds, and were the cause of his extreme unpopularity. But take him altogether he was an active, clever man, well skilled and experienced in his profession; and when his reason was not obscured by passion, few men possessed more clearness of judgement, or were more inclined to act rightly; and I believe the first impulse of General Craufurd's heart was kindness, but as he never made any attempt to control his passions the least opposition made that kindness vanish, and in its stead violence, harshness, and hatred ruled his feelings in spite of himself.

But he is gone, and as his latter life was evidently much improved and his temper more mild to those under his command, we have a right to conclude he would ere long have mastered his passions. But as a glorious death put a period to his career let his faults and errors be buried with his earthly remains. His good qualities and his gallantry will ever live in the minds of those who served under him in Spain. In a day or two after his death he was buried with military honours at the foot of the small breach where he had received his mortal wound.

As Lord Wellington (who, by-the-by, was made marquis for the taking of this fortress) had positively ordered that every wounded officer should be removed from the town to a village about thirteen miles from Ciudad Rodrigo, it was necessary, as I was the only officer still remaining there, that I should be carried in a blanket by eight or ten men as I was too ill to bear a cart. The troops being all drawn up to receive the body of General Craufurd I had to pass through them, and as I went through my own regiment I was greeted by many a kind look and exclamation of approbation and pity from the men who had so gallantly supported me in the assault. Nothing is so sweet, so soothing to a wounded officer as the homely expressions of approval and admiration which he receives from the soldiers.

You may, perhaps, laugh at it, but it made me cry with pleasure and joy to find myself among the *men*, and to see their rough, weather-beaten countenances look at me with every expression of kindly feeling. I could read their thoughts, and it made me ready to jump out of the '*brancard*' with enthusiasm. The day was intensely hot, although the month of February, and by the time I arrived at my journey's end my poor bearers and myself were completely knocked up. I was so ill and delirious that night that the surgeons thought I should have died. A few days restored my strength, but what most contributed to my recovery was a visit from Lord Wellington, who brought me the English newspapers; told me my battalion (the 2nd of the 52nd) was ordered home and that I should go also and see my mother; that he was highly pleased with my conduct, and had in consequence recommended me for the medal which would be struck upon the occasion, and also for the rank of lieutenant-colonel.

This last was joyful news for me. Lord Wellington had also written to my mother respecting me. That letter is with her papers; I have read it, and very kind and flattering it is.[2] I thanked him for all his kindness, and he then took his leave, but often repeated his visits as long as I remained near him; and I assure you, no commander ever felt more for his officers and men than the Duke of Wellington; and whenever you hear anyone say the contrary, never believe a word of it. He never failed to visit his sick and wounded when it was possible for him to do so, that is, when he had time to spare from other matters of more immediate importance, and he was more anxious about the comfort and wants of the sick than almost any other thing. His regulations were excellent, and he was particularly severe when he heard of, or found, the least want of zealous performance of their duty in the Medical Department of the army, which, it must be acknowledged, was very

2. See Appendix No. 2.

seldom the case.

About three weeks after the loss of my arm I commenced my journey towards Lisbon. The first day I left my room I mounted my horse and rode sixteen miles in a hot sun, and in a few days arrived at Coimbra, where I found my friend Colonel Colborne in bed suffering dreadful pain from his wound, while, comparatively, I was not suffering anything. Here we stayed some time, till Colborne was able to travel by easy journeys to Lisbon. When we arrived there he was so ill and weak that it was impossible he could undergo the fatigue of the voyage, so I embarked in the *Agincourt*, 74, commanded by Captain Kent, and after being sick and miserable for upwards of six weeks, I landed at Plymouth and proceeded to London to my mother's house, where, you may be sure, I was most affectionately received.

Chapter 6

Rejoin the 52nd at St. Jean de Luz

[*Note.* After spending a few months in London Lieut.-Colonel Napier went to Edinburgh, where he married the daughter of John Craig, Esq. (sister of the young William Craig already mentioned in this narrative), and was soon after appointed deputy adjutant-general to the Yorkshire District, and was quartered at York. His narrative is resumed at this point.]

After remaining at York about eight months I became effective major in the 1st battalion 52nd Regiment, which battalion being in Spain, it was necessary to join immediately. This was a severe blow to my poor wife, who did not expect to part so soon; but as she loved me with a pure and ardent affection she was as anxious about my honour and fame as I was myself, and never for one moment let me see or be aware of what misery she endured, for fear of its having any influence with me or making me waver for a moment in my determination to join the army in Spain, although I had received a letter, by the Duke of York's command, from the adjutant-general permitting me to remain upon the staff at home, as his Royal Highness considered the loss of my arm entitled me to do so.

But my wife well knew my sentiments upon that point and how strongly I had censured others for not joining their regiments, so she made up her mind to bear it as a soldier's wife ought to do, and from that moment her firmness and conduct was as perfect as any woman's could be, though her poor heart was heavy enough, God knows! But being a person of extraordinary strength of mind, she held to her resolution of acting as she thought was most conducive to her husband's honour and military character, and thereby saved me much vexation and pain; for had she tried by her influence over me to persuade me to take advantage of the Duke of York's kind permission to remain where I was, although she certainly would have failed, the love I had for her and the knowledge of her misery would have driven me half distracted.

Upon leaving her as it was, God knows, I suffered deeply! I am more particular in mentioning all these details that you, my dearest girls, if you marry soldiers or sailors, may follow your mother's bright example, and, like her, never permit your feelings so much to get the better of your duty as to influence or try to influence your husbands in acting contrary to what their honour, their character, and the duties of their profession point out as the course they should pursue; and you, boys, when you marry, recollect that although bitter will be the pain of parting with the wife you love, your duty to your country is the primary object of a soldier and to it all other feelings must give way. Neither wife, child, nor parent must stand in the way of duty as long as you wear *a red coat*, and during war you can wear no other, unless you feel you are unfit for it from *fear*, or weakness of nerves, and then the sooner you quit it the better. But of that I have no uneasiness; you have spirit enough, thank God!

On the 1st January, 1814, I went to Falmouth; embarked, encountered a severe gale of wind, and was nearly lost; but in five days from the time I left London carrying despatches to Lord Wellington I delivered them to his lordship at St. Jean de Luz in the Pyrenees. The next day I left headquarters, and arrived at the cantonments of the Light Division, where I found my friend Colborne in command of a brigade, and in consequence I had the command of the regiment, to my very great satisfaction. Here we remained a few weeks till the rains were over, which are so constant and heavy at that season in the Basque country that all the roads are rendered impracticable for any army to march on, and consequently we were forced to remain quiet.

While here, Lord March came and asked my advice about joining the regiment, in which he was a captain, in order to learn his duty practically as a Light Infantry officer, he having been always on the staff of Lord Wellington. I strongly advised him to do so, and he took my advice like a good soldier as he ever proved himself to be. Just before the weather cleared up and we were in daily expectation of advancing a senior officer to Colonel Colborne joined the division, so he lost the command of the brigade and I that of the regiment. In consequence of this Sir Edward Pakenham, the adjutant-general of the army and my intimate friend, spoke to Lord Wellington to place me on the general staff, and I was much surprised at seeing myself in orders as assistant adjutant-general to the 6th division.

This being quite unsolicited by me was very kind and flattering in the commander-in-chief and Sir Edward Pakenham; but I did not like leaving my old regiment and the Light Division, where I was certain of seeing all the fighting that might take place, so I wrote to beg leave to decline the situation, and this being acquiesced in, though not without a good deal of correspondence and remonstrance upon the part of my sincere and kind friend Sir Edward, I remained as second in command of the regiment, most of my friends thinking me very foolish to give up so good a staff appointment. My reason for it was that the great object of my wishes was to get the command of a Light Infantry regiment, and I knew that the best way to qualify myself for it was by doing regimental duty in the regiment and the division I was then in.

I also knew that the Duke of York wished officers to remain with their regiments, and that by doing so his Royal Highness would be more inclined to give me the command I wished than if I went upon the staff; and I was right, for I received a very flattering letter from the duke's secretary, Colonel Torrens, written by his command, to inform me that he was highly pleased with my declining the staff situation and remaining with my regiment; that he wished so good an example was more followed, and that his Royal Highness would take the first opportunity of showing his sense of my conduct. My kind and valued friend Sir Edward Pakenham was at first vexed with me, but as anger never entered the breast of that most delightful of all characters, he very quickly forgave me; and as I shall not have another opportunity of mentioning him, I must here describe him.

Sir Edward Pakenham was one of England's best and bravest soldiers. Bred in the army from a boy, he was early in life promoted to the command of a regiment, and was *twice* shot through the neck commanding his regiment in action in the West Indies, where he highly distinguished himself as a skilful and gallant officer long before he joined the army under the command of his brother-in-law Lord Wellington. He became adjutant-general of the army immediately upon the fall of Ciudad Rodrigo, as General Stewart (Marquis of Londonderry) went home at that period and never returned to the Peninsula, being employed elsewhere. Sir Edward proved highly useful in correcting the various disorders and want of discipline which had crept into the army (for Lord Londonderry was not a very strict adjutant-general), and enforcing the orders of Lord Wellington, which, though most excellent, had been often evaded or neglected.

Sir E. Pakenham was one of the most candid, generous, honourable, active, and intelligent general officers in the service, thoroughly acquainted with every branch of it, and having served both in the infantry and cavalry no one could impose upon him, and although one of the best-tempered men breathing he was severely strict if he perceived the slightest negligence or want of discipline. His love, zeal, and admiration for the profession of which he was one of the brightest ornaments surpassed everything imaginable, and the whole object of his life was to uphold its glory and respectability. For this he first neglected his own health in the Peninsula, and afterwards sacrificed his valuable life at New Orleans in America!

At one time he had the command of a division after the Battle of Salamanca, and distinguished himself as much in that command as he had in every situation he was placed in, and by his skilful conduct baffled the operations of one of Napoleon's best generals, Clausel, now a marshal of France. I saw him the day before he left England to command the army before New Orleans, which it was proposed to capture notwithstanding its great strength and the difficulty of getting an army before the place. He told me he hoped he should be successful, but that he much doubted the policy of the expedition or the correctness of the information upon which the government had decided to make an attempt upon that place; but that he would do all that activity, zeal, and the experience and abilities he possessed were capable of, and if he failed it should not be his fault.

I could not help begging of him to recollect that as the commander-in-chief of an army he ought not to expose himself as much as he was accustomed to do in action, for he was remarkable for always being in front, and generally wounded. I shall never forget either his reply or the look with which it was accompanied. He said, fixing his expressive eyes upon me, 'George, my good friend, I promise you that I will not unnecessarily expose myself to the fire of the enemy, but you are too old and good a soldier not to be aware that a case may arise in which the commander-in-chief may find it absolutely necessary to place himself at the head of his troops in the hottest fire and by his own personal conduct encourage them to victory. If this happens I must not flinch, though certain death be my lot!'

I never saw him again! The very case occurred by the base and cowardly conduct of ———, commanding the —— Regiment, which fled, and in rallying it and leading the troops on by his own courageous conduct, the generous, the high-minded and gallant Pakenham fell in the front of battle, a victim to the dastardly cowardice of a British officer. He was succeeded in the command by another friend of mine, a character nearly the counterpart of himself—Lieut.-General Sir Samuel Gibbs—and he also fell in the same effort to rally the flying regiment.

Thus England lost two of her best and brightest soldiers, almost at the same moment, by the cowardice of a fellow who was a disgrace to the name of Briton, and who, to the shame of the court-martial which afterwards tried him in Ireland, got off with only being *cashiered* instead of being *hung*, for shooting would have been far too honourable a death for the cowardly scoundrel! But enough of this catastrophe, by which I lost two valued friends, and let me return to where I left off.

As soon as the rainy season had a little abated we were put in movement, as Lord Wellington was determined to give Soult no rest. We made a delightful march through a most beautiful country about Pau and had famous quarters in the Basque towns and villages, where we got plenty to eat and drink; and as we paid well the people were very civil and even kind, for they looked upon us as the harbingers of *peace*, Napoleon's star being on the wane. Besides, the whole French nation was tired of war, endless war! particularly as '*la belle France*' was full of foreign enemies of all nations and her citizens now felt at their own doors the horrid evils of war, and suffered in proportion as they had devastated other countries, by whose armies France was now in her turn scourged on every side. Formerly Napoleon had kept her free from the horrors or effects of war, and had made the unfortunate nations that he conquered not only feed, clothe, and pay his soldiers, but likewise levied heavy contributions on them in order to relieve France from the burden and expenses of his wars.

Battle of Orthez

At Orthez, a town in France about twenty miles from Pau, we came up with Marshal Soult's army, which was posted on a long range of very high ground, with a large plain in its rear over which passed the roads to Bayonne, Bordeaux, and Toulouse; and in front of the enemy's position and immediately in its centre was a deep marsh through which ran a small rivulet, but of no note—indeed, in summer it is dry. On the right was a village in which Soult had placed a very heavy column of infantry and artillery. This he considered the key of his position, as he did not fear for his front or centre in consequence of the marshy ground. His left was just above the town of Orthez, which he held, and here he had placed General Foy with a strong force also. Our army, which had passed the river during the morning at various fords (and which I am surprised that Soult permitted us to do so easily), had assembled in different columns, waiting the order of attack.

General Picton's column was on the right, facing the enemy's left; the Light Division, consisting principally of the 52nd Regiment (as the 43rd had gone to the rear for clothing), was to attack the centre of the French in line; and General Cole commanded the left column which was to attack the village already mentioned on the enemy's right. While we were waiting for the signal to attack I happened to be near Lord Wellington who was observing the enemy with his telescope, and perceiving an alteration in Marshal Soult's movements, he immediately altered the plan of his own attack and ordered the 52nd Regiment to form line and march straight through the marsh and attack the centre of the enemy's position without delay. In a few minutes we were in full march, up to our knees every step in the bog, the enemy pouring a heavy and well-directed fire upon us from the height above, which we could not return.

I never saw our fellows behave more steadily or more gallantly; but, owing to the ground, our line was not very *correct*. My horse floundered in the bog, and in spite of all my spurring and Lord March's beating and kicking him, we could not make the poor brute stir, so I was obliged to leave him to my servant and take his. At last we made the enemy retire and gained the brow of the hill, and then dressed our line and commenced a heavy rolling fire in our turn, advancing at the same time. During our advance through the bog the left and right of our army attacked, but made no impression; indeed our left column of attack under Sir Lowry Cole was driven back several times and suffered severely, the enemy being in great force in the village and much too strongly placed for our people to force them from their position.

However, when Marshal Soult found that our regiment had succeeded in gaining the centre of his position and was steadily advancing, he gave orders for retreating, which was done in the best order possible; and as night very soon came on, we gave up the pursuit and bivouacked. And thus ended the battle of Orthez, without much loss on either side—I suppose not twelve hundred on our part, and perhaps a few hundred more on that of the French—except that we took great numbers of conscripts prisoners.

Just before we had completely driven the French from their position I had ridden to the right of our regiment, when Lord March, who was a captain in it and had joined from Lord Wellington's staff, came up to me and said, 'George, you see I am not hit yet though you swore I should be as soon as I left the staff and joined my regiment,' alluding to a joke of mine a few days before. I answered, 'Do not holloa till you're out of the wood; the action is not over yet, my Lord March.'

I had not gone a hundred paces when a sergeant came running after me, saying, 'Oh, sir, Lord March is killed!' I went to him, and found my gallant, high-spirited, young friend lying with his head in my brother William's lap, to all appearance a lifeless corpse. I was deeply shocked; I dismounted from my horse; I kissed his forehead, and took his cold hand in mine; but my duty called me elsewhere, and I left him with my brother (whose regiment was not in action and he was therefore at leisure), in the full persuasion that I had parted with him forever.

However, thank God, I was wrong, for he recovered—though the ball is to this day in his chest—and was sufficiently well to join us at Toulouse, to the great joy of the 52nd Regiment, the Light Division, and I may say the whole army, for he was known by all, and to know Lord March was sufficient to love him. It was impossible for any young man to be more popular, or to deserve it better, both as a gentleman and a soldier.

I must here mention an anecdote which was told me by the best authority—one of the persons concerned. Lord March was conveyed to the town of Orthez to a quarter there, as it was made the hospital for the wounded. The next night after he was wounded he was in so dangerous a state that Dr. Hare of the 43rd, who attended him, had given positive orders that no noise should be made and that as he should himself remain up all night with Lord March, if anyone wanted to come into the room they should not speak, but be as quiet as possible.

About the middle of the night, as Dr. Hare was sitting dozing in a chair opposite Lord March's bed, who had fallen asleep, the door of the room gently opened and a figure in a white cloak and military hat walked up to the bed, drew the curtains quietly aside, looked steadily for a few seconds on the pale countenance before him, then leaned over, stooped his head, and pressed his lips on the forehead of Lord March, heaved a deep sigh, and turned to leave the room, when the doctor, who had anxiously watched every movement, beheld the countenance of *Wellington!* his cheeks wet with tears. He had ridden many a mile that night, alone, to see his favourite young soldier, the son of his dearest friend. He then returned to his headquarters, having first made every inquiry respecting the sick and wounded and given such orders as were necessary. Does this betray a want of feeling in the duke? It needs no comment; the fact speaks for itself.

Next morning we pursued the French Army, and General Hill's corps, which had passed higher up than the town of Orthez, came up with a part of the enemy at Aire, between Pau and Mont-de-Marsan, and immediately attacking drove them from their position. In a day or two we again came in contact with our enemy at Tarbes on the Toulouse road. Here the Light Division had a slight skirmish and drove a French brigade from their position on a woody hill; but it was done without loss on our part and scarcely any on that of the French; just a spirt of a moment to enliven us a little after some hours of a hot dusty march.

The cavalry and sharpshooters of some of the other divisions had a *petite affaire* nearer the town of Tarbes, on our right, in which an old friend of ours was killed—Colonel Sturgeon—I may safely say one of the cleverest and most clear-headed, experienced officers in the British Army, and a man in whom Lord Wellington had the highest confidence and whose opinion (if he ever took any man's in preference to his own, which I doubt) he is said to have often asked and sometimes followed. But be that as it may, Sturgeon was held in high estimation by every officer in that army, and all deeply lamented his loss, the more particularly because a short time before he had been harshly treated by Lord Wellington, and was very severely reprimanded by his Lordship in presence of a number of officers who were at dinner at headquarters.

The thing was thus. Lord Wellington had made Sturgeon superintendent of the post-office and despatch department of the army, and also commandant of the Corps of Guides and Couriers, which it was of the utmost importance to keep in a constant state of readiness. The pay was very high, and the duke, from his confidence in and general liking for Colonel Sturgeon, put all these departments under him; at the same time he permitted him to be on the quartermaster-general's staff at headquarters, and he was also major in the staff corps; so that his pecuniary emoluments were greater than those of any other man of his rank in the army, which no man envied, as he was so highly esteemed and looked up to both as a gentleman and an officer.

Well, after the Battle of Orthez, and a force having been sent under very peculiar circumstances towards Bordeaux, the duke having written his despatches for England, with an account of the battle, and also having others for Sir John Hope, who was blockading the fortress of Bayonne and with whom it was of the utmost importance to communicate, called for the couriers and guides who were to carry them, or rather to accompany the officers from relay to relay, when to his astonishment poor Sturgeon (who had totally forgotten all about them, being full of the grand movements of the army) had not a single courier or guide ready, nor indeed knew anything about them; neither had he made the slightest arrangement for the communications of the army, and his corps of guides had gone where they pleased. He could tell nothing about them, and in consequence the despatches were delayed several days!

This made Lord Wellington furious, and he was so violent in his manner and harsh in his expressions that poor Sturgeon sunk completely under it, and a few days afterwards took the opportunity of the affair at Tarbes to gallop in among the enemy's skirmishers and got shot through the head! That the commander-in-chief had sore cause to complain and was justly angry I deny not; but I cannot help regretting that he should have publicly and severely reprimanded so distinguished an officer for his first and only fault, and I still more regret that Lord Wellington, after Sturgeon's death, should in his despatch merely say, 'Colonel Sturgeon of the Staff Corps was killed by the enemy's sharpshooters,' thus leaving the merits and distinguished long, and faithful services of a gallant and skilful soldier unrecorded or unadorned by his praise, when his censure was such that the wounded spirit of this honourable man sought refuge in the arms of death, I am sure Lord Wellington felt it afterwards, and deeply too; but he has always kept to that system of never acknowledging he was wrong or mistaken.

After the business of Tarbes we pursued the French, who went off in the direction of Toulouse, which town they reached sometime early in May; and having long before prepared everything for its defence and formed an entrenched camp, Marshal Soult determined to give us battle under the walls of the ancient capital of the South of France. It is necessary here to state that during our march very few, if any, outrages were committed by the British troops, or Portuguese; but the Spaniards, under General Morillo, plundered and ravaged the country wherever they were quartered. Wellington did all he could to prevent it; but I must say I cannot see that the Spaniards were so much to blame as people think. How was it possible for these men to forget all the oppression, plunder, and cruelties which the French Army had committed upon them and their country? No! Of course they panted for revenge, and retaliated the moment it was in their power. I *regret* that they did so, but am not surprised; indeed, I should have been astonished had they done otherwise.

Of course, the contrast between them and the Portuguese in this matter was very striking and glorious to that army, as I believe there was not an instance of a Portuguese soldier having committed a crime of any importance from their entry into France to the hour they left it on their return to Spain. However, we must take into consideration that they had a large number of British officers in all their regiments, and that they were nearly all under the command of Englishmen and were mixed with the British Army in the various divisions and brigades. As we marched through France I was surprised to see the depredations committed by the *French* Army on their retreat and to hear the curses and execrations lavished upon them by their own people; and indeed they deserved it, for they showed very little compunction in robbing and pillaging every farm and village they passed, and the inhabitants told me they paid for nothing but took whatever was necessary.

On the arrival of the British Army on the banks of the Garonne we went into famous quarters in the several small villages which are so prettily scattered about the neighbourhood of Toulouse. Part of the army had been detached under Lord Dalhousie to Bordeaux, as the inhabitants of that city had declared themselves in favour of the Bourbons, and had hoisted the '*drapeau blanc*.' This, and the portion of the army under Sir John Hope left to blockade the fortress and port of Bayonne, had reduced Lord Wellington's forces at Toulouse to a much smaller number than when he entered France in one large body; and this has given rise to an idea that he was nearly double the strength of Marshal Soult's army, which is very far from the truth, as I think he could not have had more than thirty-five thousand men, seven or eight thousand of whom were Spaniards, the rest British and Portuguese.

The French acknowledge to twenty-two or-three thousand in an entrenched position, and well supported by forts, &c. Every means of defence possible was at Soult's command, as the town itself made part of his position; so that the three or four thousand we had over his numbers were amply compensated for by the different position of the armies, and the circumstance of our being the attacking and his the defensive one. That he ably placed his army, and gallantly and skilfully fought the battle, I deny not; but that he won it, as the French assert, is not true. Every fort was taken, his divisions driven into the town, and the British Army bivouacked upon the field of battle, and the next day entered the town which he had evacuated during the night.

Battle of Toulouse

The Duke of Wellington's first intention had been to cross the Garonne above the town of Toulouse, and he had accordingly been making every preparation for so doing. The pontoons for the bridge had arrived, and all being reported ready, we moved in separate columns towards the spot decided upon, when, lo! the engineer had miscalculated the breadth of the river, and had not ordered up a sufficient number of pontoons to lay the bridge and we were obliged to abandon the project, as, the enemy being now aware of our intention, it would not be possible to throw a bridge across at that spot. Lord Wellington was furious. I never saw him in such a rage, and no wonder; for this unpardonable mistake was the cause of many days' delay, and forced us to cross lower down below the town, where the river was wider, deeper, and much more rapid and the difficulties much greater than at the other place.

When the new bridge was finished the fourth division, a part of the sixth, and a brigade of hussars—the whole under General Cole—crossed over, and after driving in the enemy's outposts and having an affair of cavalry, bivouacked in front of the enemy's position, but at some distance. We were all to have passed over also, when a sudden storm came on and a deluge of rain, which so swelled the river that it carried away our pontoons and destroyed the bridge completely, and left the troops which had passed over totally unsupported in case of an attack. And why Soult allowed them to remain unmolested for three days, which it took to make a new bridge, I cannot conceive. All his generals begged and prayed him to attack and, as they said, annihilate this small force; but he would not run the risk, and (as I have understood from many French officers) said, 'You do not know what stuff two British divisions are made of; they would not be conquered as long as there was a man of them left to stand, and I cannot afford to lose men now.'

When the bridge was ready we all passed over as quickly as possible, and next day attacked the French in their position. The 4th, 6th, and a Portuguese division under Marshal Beresford's orders, attacked the great fort on the right of the French, and here was the brunt of the battle, for the enemy was strongly posted and flanked by works, with trenches in their front, and their best troops opposed to ours. But nothing could damp the courage of this column; the enemy's guns poured a torrent of fire upon it; still it moved onward, when column upon column appeared, crowning the hill and forming lines in front and on the flanks of our brave fellows who were near the top; and then such a roll of musketry accompanied by peals of cannon and the shouts of the enemy commenced, that our soldiers were fairly forced to give way and were driven down again.

This attack was twice renewed, and twice were our gallant fellows forced to retire, when, being got into order again and under a tremendous fire of all arms from the enemy, they once more marched onward determined 'to do or die' (for they were nearly all Scotch) and, having gained the summit of the position, they charged with the bayonet, and in spite of every effort of the enemy, drove all before them and entered every redoubt and fort with such a courage as I never saw before. The enemy lay in *heaps*, dead and dying! Few, very few, escaped the slaughter of that day; but 'victory' was heard shouted from post to post as that gallant band moved along the crown of the enemy's position taking every work at the point of the bayonet.

While the work of death was going on here, the centre of the French position was attacked by the Spanish column of eight thousand men, under General Freyre, who had *demanded* in rather a haughty tone that Lord Wellington should give the Spaniards the post of honour in the battle. He acceded, but took special care to have the Light Division in reserve to support them in case of *accidents*. Old Freyre placed himself at the head of his column, surrounded by his staff, and marched boldly up the hollow way, or road, which led right up to the enemy, under a heavy and destructive fire of cannon shot, which plunging into the head of his column made great havoc among his men; still they went steadily and boldly on, to my astonishment and delight to see them behave so gallantly, and I could not help expressing my delight to Colonel Colborne.

But, alas! he knew them too well, and said to me 'Gently, my friend; don't praise them too soon; look at yonder brigade of French Light Infantry, ready to attack them as soon as the head of their column enters the open ground. One moment more and we shall see the Spaniards fly! Gallop off, you, and throw the 52nd Regiment (which was in line) into open column of companies, and let these fellows pass through, or they will carry the regiment off with them.' He had scarcely finished the words when a well-directed fire from the French Infantry opened upon the Spanish column, and instantly the words '*Vive l'Empereur! En avant! en avant!*' accompanied by a charge, put the Spaniards to flight, and down they came upon the 52nd Regiment, and I had but just time to throw it into open column of companies when they rushed through the intervals like a torrent and never stopped till they arrived at the river some miles in the rear.

As soon as they had passed, and I had formed the regiment into line again, we moved up and took the Spaniards' place, driving before us the enemy's brigade, who, being by this time completely beaten on the right and all his forts and trenches carried by Beresford's troops, had retreated into the town; so that we found the fort on that part of the position which we attacked quite abandoned, and we entered it without loss.

On our right the 3rd Division, under General Picton, was ordered to make a false attack on the canal bridge, which was strongly fortified and formed an impracticable barrier to that part of the town; but General Picton (who never hesitated at disobeying his orders) thought proper to change this false attack into a real one, and after repeated and useless attempts to carry it was forced to give it up, with an immense loss of officers and men. To our extreme right and on the opposite side of the river General Hill was stationed with his corps in order to watch the bridge and gates of the town, and either prevent any attempt of the enemy to pass over a body of troops during the action to cut off our communications with the rear, or, should he show any design of retreating that way. to impede him. However, all was quiet on that side, and now that every man of the enemy's army had been chased from the position the battle was won, and the roar of cannon, the fire of the musketry, and the shouts of the victors ceased.

All was still; the pickets placed; the sentinels set; and the greatest part of the army sleeping in groups round the fires of the bivouac. I must here say that Marshal Beresford performed his part nobly that day; for had he not shown great determination and presence of mind in renewing his attacks so often and leading the troops so gallantly himself the thing might not have been so successful. But, to be sure, 'Old Douro' (as the men always called him) was on the ground himself and gave all the orders, and on him alone rested any responsibility, so that Marshal Beresford was relieved from that burden, which is a heavy one to those who have not full confidence in themselves under all circumstances; and it is better for a man to act wrong, if he does so with confidence in himself, than be hesitating or doubtful of what he ought to do.

And if ever any of you, boys, become a general and have a command, never be foolish enough to call a *council of war*, for of all evils in the army that is the *very worst*. Act for yourself, and on your own responsibility; never fear the result. There are people who will, and do, hold another doctrine, but they are wrong, rely upon it. I never saw, or read, or heard of a general who, being afraid to act for himself and called a council of war, did not fail completely. You should commence your life as a soldier with the determination to act for yourself, and to trust to no man for that which you can do yourself; and bear in your mind the motto, '*Aut Caesar aut nullus.*' Always keep that in view and you will succeed.

This was the last and one of the bloodiest battles fought by that army under its great commander Wellington, who after seven years' hard struggle with the most powerful nation in Europe for the liberty of the Peninsula, put a period to the war by a glorious victory in the heart of France, bearing the British flag on the wings of victory from the shores of the Tagus to the towers of Toulouse, where it waved, the emblem of British honour and the avenger of Iberia's wrongs! Had the Duke of Wellington never drawn his sword again or fought another battle this alone would have ranked him among the ablest generals of his time, for although Waterloo was certainly one of the bloodiest victories ever won, against the ablest general in the world, and the result the total over-throw of the most extraordinary man that history tells of, still I say the Duke of Wellington's military fame must, and will, rest upon his Peninsular campaigns, in which one is at a loss what to admire the most—his determination never to abandon his own views, but to persevere and struggle against every difficulty and impediment at home and abroad—to depend upon his army and himself alone—to baffle or defeat by his forethought and military skill every effort of a wily enemy as daring as himself—to despise public clamour—to make his country's glory his landmark in every enterprise—to encourage the ardour of his troops by impartial justice and by promoting those who deserved it—to advance or to *retreat* when prudence dictated it, in spite of the malicious taunts of a free press, or an ignorant and factious opposition—and to fight only when necessity or the science of war required it, caring little for the personal glory reflecting on himself, but looking to its effects on the great and ultimate object of his ambition, namely, driving the French armies out of the Peninsula, and liberating the Spanish nation from the yoke of France.

All this did he accomplish, and thus stamped his character as one of the greatest captains that ever lived; and he is now gaining civic laurels in still greater abundance by passing the Catholic question, and thereby giving freedom and tranquillity to long-oppressed and deeply-injured Ireland.[1] Long may he live, and long may he be at the head of the first nation in the world, is the present prayer of every true Englishman, be he soldier, sailor, or civilian.

---

1. This, it must be remembered, was written in 1828.—Ed. (W.N.)

Chapter 7

Sail for England

A few days after the Battle of Toulouse I was appointed regimental lieutenant-colonel of the 71st Light Infantry, and immediately took the command of it, superseding ———, who had been dismissed the service for cowardly conduct in the field, in leaving his regiment in action and going to the rear, where unluckily for him but luckily for the regiment and the service, Lord Wellington who was coming up, met him and reprimanding him on the spot told him to go back instantly and head his gallant regiment. Go back he did, but head the regiment, never in action! and Lord Wellington having reported his conduct to his Royal Highness the Duke of York, the Prince Regent dismissed him from the army, and I was gazetted in his place. He was a man of large fortune and a very old officer, just upon the point of being made by brevet a major-general, but he was weak, overbearing, and insolent beyond everything to all under him in rank, and by his conduct to the officers of his regiment had nearly extinguished the honourable spirit which had so long and so highly distinguished it under his predecessors, Sir Denis Pack and Colonel Cadogan.

In short, to ———, and to him alone, belonged all the disorder which the 71st Regiment got into after poor Colonel Cadogan's glorious death at the Battle of Vittoria; the proof of which was that in the course of a few months after I took the command we received the thanks and approbation of the general commanding the division, Sir William Stewart, for its good conduct and high state of discipline. This I mention as a proof that the regiment's being in bad order was ———'s sole fault, for had I been the cleverest commanding officer in the army it would have been impossible for me in so short a period, and under the circumstances of the time, to have made the progress I did if it had not been for the former system established by Pack and

Cadogan, which I found was still in the regiment, but, from the conduct of ———, had been totally neglected and almost forgotten; and I soon saw I had only to be firm, impartial, and strict in enforcing my orders but with calmness and temper, and that I should in a short time bring all back to its former splendour.

In this I succeeded, but not without some severity, for I found the discipline so relaxed that neither officers nor men were very well inclined to submit cheerfully to my orders, which were looked upon as too strict; and I am sorry to say I was forced to make some severe examples by flogging more men in the first two months I was with the 71st than I had witnessed or ordered during nearly as many years in the 52nd! However, by constant hard work of body and mind, night and day, and by repeatedly assembling the officers and impressing upon them the necessity of regaining their former character, which could only be accomplished by incessant and zealous attention upon their part to every duty however trifling, I at last succeeded, and I never saw a finer set of young men, or officers who did their duty with a higher feeling of honour, zeal, and cheerful activity.

When the men perceived that the officers were determined to support me, and I them, and to do their duty to the utmost, and, above all, that I was neither to be frightened nor trifled with, and never went back from my word either in rewards or punishments, they also took a new turn after seeing that the anonymous letters I received in quantities every day to tell me they would take an opportunity of shooting me if I went on so severely had no effect, and that I told them I would give any of them an opportunity to try it night or day, and ordered the sentinel at my door to be taken off so that there should be no hindrance to any man to enter my room for that purpose; but I also told them that the man who did attempt it would perhaps not come off so easily as he might think, as although I had but one hand it was pretty strong, and well able to use either sword or pistol, neither of which would they ever find me without!

From this time all went well, and I had scarcely ever a fault to find with man or officer; and from the manner in which they expressed themselves to me upon my leaving the regiment, and what I was afterwards told by many officers, I am proud to say I was sincerely regretted by all of them: but it was no '*bed of roses*' for the first two months. Now, boys, I will tell you the secret how to command a regiment (if ever you are in so honourable and so enviable a position). It is this. Be *just* and perfectly impartial in your conduct to officers and privates;

never permit any person, whatever may be his rank or character, to disobey or dispute your orders upon any pretext whatever; but then on your part do not give orders of no real consequence in themselves, and which only irritate and tease others.

When you have occasion to find fault with an officer do not give way to anger or temper, neither say any harsh thing before the soldiers as that only lowers the officer in the estimation of the men; and every commanding officer should do all in his power to keep up the respectability of his officers and make the soldiers look up to them with that esteem, respect, and confidence which every good and well-conducted man is entitled to and is sure to receive from all ranks in society. When an officer has committed a fault send for him to your room, and there privately, in a cool, deliberate, and friendly manner, lecture him upon his conduct; point out to him the evil consequences of it in regard to his own character and prospects, as well as the disgrace brought upon the regiment by the misconduct of any of its members, and more particularly by an officer, whose education and principles of honour ought to teach him better.

If he offends a second time speak to him in presence of his brother officers; but should this also fail, and he is incorrigible, then you have but one course left—put him under arrest, report his conduct to the general commanding, and let him be dealt with according to the pleasure of the commander-in-chief. If a non-commissioned officer or private soldier behaves ill, speak to him in the first instance and try what impression you can make on him by advice and gentleness. If, after repeated small punishments and advice you fail to get him to behave as a good soldier, then you must resort to severity; but rely upon it that it rarely happens when a soldier is treated with kindness and the respect shown to him which is due from one man to another, that he will be insensible to such treatment and persevere in an evil course of life.

The fault generally lies with the officer who, not having carefully watched and well studied the character and dispositions of his soldiers, is far too apt to imagine that *punishment*, as it is the least trouble, is the only way to keep soldiers in order; and by at once ordering punishment the soldier is disgraced for a slight crime, rendered careless and reckless of his future conduct, and, from disgust and sulkiness at severe treatment, becomes a bad soldier and a worse man. Therefore I hold that the first and greatest duty an officer has to perform is that of *preventing* crime in the soldier, and the surest and most honourable means of doing so is to look upon the soldier as a fellow-citizen, who, being by the admitted laws of society and for the general good of the State placed under you in rank and station, is nevertheless as good a man and as good a Christian as yourself, born in the same country, amenable to the same laws, and above all possessing the same feelings as the proudest peer in the land.

In short, recollect that a time must inevitably come when the officer and private, the peasant and the peer, will alike have to render their account of their conduct in this world to the same Great Author of our existence who made all men equal in His sight, and to whose impartial justice neither rank nor birth will be an excuse for the ill-treatment of a fellow-creature. There are, however, some military crimes which, for the general good of society and the absolute necessity of keeping up the discipline of the army, cannot be lightly looked over or pardoned.

These are, or will be ere long I trust, so completely and clearly defined that the punishment of them will never depend on the whim or caprice of any officer however exalted his rank; and when the soldier is fully aware before he enters the army that there are certain crimes, and those no light ones, which must lead to punishment without a possibility of escape, they will seldom be committed; and if a plan which my friend Sir Henry Hardinge, the Secretary at War, has been so kind as to show me, is brought to perfection and adopted, I look forward with pleasure and certainty to a period arriving when a British soldier will never have his back bared to the lash of the cat-o'-nine-tails! and Sir Henry Hardinge will be justly honoured, not only by the gratitude of the army, but also by that of the nation. [1]

Many people have a notion that Marshal Soult knew of the overthrow of Napoleon, and that the peace was signed before he fought the Battle of Toulouse; but I think this must be a calumny invented by his enemies, and I feel the more convinced of this because it was against his interest and fame to have done so if he could have avoided it. Had he abstained from fighting he would have remained in the military possession of the town and all the district upon the right bank of the Garonne, which it was his interest to keep, and thereby kept us out of the capital of the south of France; instead of which he was beaten by the British army, leaving the Duke of Wellington in possession of Toulouse and all the country on both banks of the river from that city

---

1. Sir Henry Hardinge has, I am sorry to say, left the War Office, and I doubt if ever there will be found a man equal to him in that situation.

to Bordeaux. Besides, it was Lord Wellington who attacked *him*.

In a few weeks we received orders to prepare for returning to England, but before the army began to move we learned that a large force was to embark at Bordeaux for America, in order to finish the war with the United States, which had been rather unfavourable to our arms; the rest were to embark for England and Ireland, while the cavalry marched through France for Calais, in order to save the horses so long a voyage by sea. I was left with my regiment to remain in Toulouse for some days after the whole army had marched, in order to bring up the rear and clear the country of all stragglers and followers of the army, sick, stores, &c., &c.; in short, to drive the 'tag, rag, and bob-tail' before me. I had a very pleasant march (though dreadfully hot) through the south of France; everywhere receiving the greatest kindness and civility from the inhabitants.

In almost every town we passed the night they gave us a ball, where we met all the ladies, and my officers made themselves agreeable, dancing the whole night. I had but *one complaint* during our long march against our men, and that was on the second day's march, when a woman came to my quarters at the mayor's house, and, crying and tearing her hair and wringing her hands, and accompanied by a mob of people, all talking and swearing that the soldiers were going to rob and murder the people and set fire to the town, she called on me for protection and justice. I, not knowing the nature of the French, supposed there was the devil to pay, so immediately demanding from *madame* what my soldiers had done, she answered, 'Stole an old hen from her yard.' 'Oh, oh,' said I to myself, 'is that all? thank God it's no worse,' and I ordered my orderly bugleman to sound the assembly, and told the lady she should go down the ranks of the regiment and point out the soldier who had committed the theft, as she said she would know him directly again.

As soon as the regiment was formed, which was in about a quarter of an hour from her first coming to complain, I took her down the ranks, and upon coming opposite a company which I expected the fellow belonged to, she at once pointed him out. I asked him if he stole her hen; he resolutely denied knowing anything of the matter; upon which I ordered him to take off his knapsack and open it, when, sure enough, there was the old hen, dead as a *ducat*, with all her feathers on, so that the lady could swear to it. I instantly ordered a drum-head court-martial, tried my gentleman on the spot, and as he was proved guilty of plundering and sentenced to be flogged, I punished him accordingly before them all; and then the lady was furious with me, and all the people begged and prayed I would forgive him, and when they found I would not they abused me like a pickpocket.

Now it may be thought that I was very severe and cruel in doing this, and all for an *old hen*; but my reason was this—I was left by the commander-in-chief to bring up the rear of the British Army, and to prevent all kind of irregularity or ill-treatment of the inhabitants. Therefore it was absolutely necessary that I should keep my own men in a perfect state of discipline; and had I forgiven this man, the next day there would have been *ten hens stolen*, and then probably ten *napoleons*, and so on till the men would become completely disorganised, and the inhabitants be plundered and pillaged in every direction, and the army disgraced by our conduct.

Besides I was in an awkward situation; not another regiment within five days' march of me, and all in my front, not a single man in my rear to fall back upon for support should the conduct of our men so irritate the inhabitants as to make them rise *en masse* and attack me when I had no suspicion of their hostility. All these considerations passed through my mind while the court-martial was trying the man, and I determined by a well-timed severity to crush at once all idea of or attempt at pillage, or the slightest irregularity of conduct in my regiment; and as I was sure it would, so it did prevent it, for that was the first, the last, and only act of misconduct in my men from the day we left Toulouse to the day we arrived at Bordeaux, after a march of nearly three weeks. I think it will now be seen that I was right in not forgiving the man and that the punishment served as an example to deter others.

On my arrival at Bordeaux I received letters which alarmed me about my wife's health, so I instantly went to my friends Sir Edward Pakenham and Lord Fitzroy Somerset, who got me leave to go home without waiting for my regiment, which was ordered to Ireland. After a stormy and very unpleasant passage down the river, I got on board a transport which was sailing for Plymouth; but I had a curious adventure while coming down the river. A brother officer who was with me, Colonel Charles Rowan (now the chief of the police in London, and one of the best and cleverest, gallant, honourable men in existence, as well as a staunch and true friend), and I went on shore to look at a curious village cut in the rock.

Each house was perfectly separate, but cut in the rock; bedrooms, kitchen, &c., &c., with regular communications, exactly like the inside of a house; not the least difference, except that all the rooms were in a line and looking towards the river, otherwise there would have been a want of light; but there were chambers one above the other with steps cut in the rock to enable one to get up to each storey.

As I had on my uniform, we were immediately known to be British officers, and as most of the male inhabitants were sailors just released by the peace from our prisons and hulks, where, to the eternal disgrace and shame of the British Government, they had been most infamously and inhumanly treated, they were determined to insult us, and commenced throwing stones and abusing us most desperately. So furious were they that we deemed it the most prudent thing to retreat to our boat as fast as we could. However, as I was very angry, I drew forth one of my pistols and was just going to fire at them, but Rowan, being a wiser and cooler-headed fellow, very properly prevented my doing so, and luckily for us, as in a few moments the whole village turned out, and we had but just time to regain the boat and shove out and, a breeze springing up, we made all sail into the middle of the river, which was very broad, and escaped their fury, for they certainly would have murdered us without mercy.

That night very late I was so ill from sea-sickness that I swore I would not remain any longer in the cursed boat, and Rowan very good-humouredly got out with me, and we waded up to our middle through a long mile of mud, as the tide was out; and at last, having gained the bank, we made the best of our way to a light we perceived at some distance, where finding a house we knocked at the door, which was soon opened by a nice pretty French girl, and upon our saying we were English officers, a gentleman came forward and in broken English welcomed us to his house and said we should have every accommodation he could give us.

The pretty girl smiled a good deal at our dirty muddy figures, but was very active and good-natured in getting us supper and famous wine, and the gentleman lent us some of his things while ours went through the process of cleaning and drying, and after supper we went into most excellent beds, the master of the house promising we should have his little pony chaise, and breakfast at daylight to proceed to the place off which our ships were lying at anchor. We asked him how he came to understand English, and he then said, as well as I can recollect:

Gentlemen, I was the owner of a small trading-vessel by which

I made a comfortable living, when one unfortunate day I was taken a prize to an English man-of-war, carried off with my ship, my property, and my crew to England, where, all being condemned by your Court of Admiralty as lawful prize, myself and my men were sent to the prison-ships as prisoners of war. There I received very abominable and harsh treatment, and was witness to many horrid scenes of cruelty on one side by the keepers, and depravity on the other by the unfortunate captives. I was placed in the same hold with the men because I was not an officer, only a private trader, and this treatment and captivity I endured for *nine years.*

When peace came I returned within these few weeks to my home, but owing to my absence my property has been badly and dishonestly managed, and I have not much left, or I would have given you better fare and accommodation; but I know all this was owing to the bad regulations of your government, the brutal violence of those in charge of the prisoners, and the obstinacy of Napoleon in refusing to exchange prisoners. I therefore blame not the English nation, but the government: far from it, I admire you, I think you generous, kind, and brave; and I glory in being of use to British officers, whom I know to be men of honour and gentlemen.'

It will easily be supposed how I felt and blushed at the comparison between this generous, high-minded man's treatment as a prisoner (which ought to disarm all animosity), and his treatment of us as officers of that same country, and who belonged to an army which had invaded his. I felt lowered as an Englishman, and could not help telling him so, when he again assured me that he and all intelligent Frenchmen knew and felt the difference between the English *Nation* and its *then government,* under Lord Castlereagh, to whom they attributed all that was bad.

This gentleman was no follower of Napoleon, nor indeed an admirer of him, as a rule, only as a great captain; and I seldom have met a more liberal and enlightened man than he appeared to be, I have forgotten his name, which I am very sorry for. In the morning we took leave of our kind host, and in a few hours we arrived at the place for embarking, when we saw the ships *in full sail* for England. However, I soon overtook one of the large transports in a small boat which I hired for the purpose, and in a fortnight we arrived at Plymouth after a miserable passage. During the whole time I was as sick as a dog, and lay upon the deck *night and day* without being able to move, and as it rained nearly the whole time and I had nothing to change—for I had left my servant in the boat with my baggage in the middle of the river—you may suppose I was as miserable as possible! As soon as I landed at Plymouth I bought a couple of shirts and a pair of stockings and started that day on top of the coach for London, remained a few hours with my mother and went off at night by the mail to Edinburgh, where I arrived just five days after I landed at Plymouth, and I found my dear wife much better than I expected.

We remained in Scotland some weeks, when in consequence of the recommendation of the Duke of Wellington I was given a company in the 3rd Guards as a reward for my services, it being considered a great favour and honour to be a captain in the Guards, which ranks with a commanding officer of a regiment, but in a pecuniary point is much better, as when I got my company it was worth between six and seven hundred a year. I remained in the Guards seven years, when in consequence of the most melancholy and most unfortunate event of my life, and end of my happiness, the death of my wife, I left them; and although I entered the line again as commanding the 44th Regiments, when that regiment was ordered to India I determined to go on half pay and devote myself wholly to the care and education of my young and helpless family, deprived at so early an age of that greatest of blessings, a good and fond mother!

And now, my dear children, having brought up the narrative of my life to the close of the Peninsular war, I hope you may have as much amusement in it as you expect, and that you will learn from it how much depends upon your own good conduct, sense, and judgement, in order to acquit yourselves well in whatever situation you may be placed; and you, my boys, will see that if a man has a true and high sense of *honour*, is zealous and cheerful in the performance of every duty, never deviates from the broad path of virtue, always recollecting that whatever he may try to conceal from men he cannot conceal from *God* or his own conscience, he may obtain honours, rank, and fame, and stand high in the estimation of his king and country, and after a life of active usefulness descend into the tomb respected and regretted by his relations and his friends.

CHAPTER 8

Concluding Extract

The extracts from my father's narrative should, properly, end at the last chapter, but I am induced to add the following extract in order to show the deep affection, respect, and gratitude which, in happier days, were felt by the Irish peasantry towards a good landlord, before they were misled by self-interested men under the false garb of patriotism.

******

After describing the illness and death of his aunt, Lady Louisa Conolly, my father thus continues:

Before the day came when it would be necessary to place her remains in the coffin the poor labourers and others of the town (Celbridge) wished to be allowed to see the body, to which I, of course, consented. I watched, from a recess where I could see, without being observed, the various persons as they came in singly and went to the bed where she lay, with a countenance so serene, so beautiful, that you could scarce believe she was not alive! As every poor person, after seeing her, passed on to another room and (not seeing me in the recess) conceived himself alone and unobserved, I had full opportunity of watching their natural feelings; and if ever gratitude for benefits conferred, and the deep affliction, nay, I may say despair, for the loss of a parent was depicted in the countenances of any human being, it was so in the countenances of these poor Irish Catholics!

One old white-headed man took up her cold, lifeless hand, and kissing it, on his knees, sobbed out:

'Oh, my dear, my sweet lady, my long-tried, my only friend, why have you left your poor old creature to die alone? You, that used to come to his bedside when he was sick, and cheer him up with your good word, and give him the drop of soup and the bit of meat, and tell him to have comfort; and now you're gone before me after all! But

I'll not stay long; I'll follow you, for you'll clear the way for a poor old sinner like myself, and God will receive me from you.'

Then he crossed himself, placed her hand gently down, kissed it again, and with his face streaming with tears, he tottered out of the room.

Another much younger man, after gently and in the most feeling, delicate, and respectful manner taking up her hand to kiss, knelt down in the attitude of prayer, and looking up towards heaven, with a countenance bedewed with tears but full of the most devotional expression, exclaimed aloud, The priest may tell me what he likes. He may curse the heretic, and swear the Protestant goes not to heaven; but neither priest, nor bishop, nor all the priests that ever lived, shall persuade me that my sainted lady, that lies now dead before me, is not gone to heaven and rests at peace in the bosom of a just and merciful God! No, no! If the soul of our dear, sweet Lady Louisa, the poor man's friend and comforter, is not gone to heaven, then there is no God, no mercy for the human race! Protestant, Catholic—what is it but a name? But look at her; look at the tears of the poor, the old, the young, the infirm and helpless; and, and, tell me, ye priests, if these are not her passports to heaven? Yes, you are cold and lifeless, and hear not the wailings of those whom you cherished as your children; but your bright spirit is above, and will look down upon us, who have now no friend left since you are gone.'

Various other instances I saw of this genuine feeling of love, gratitude, and deep sorrow for the loss of their friend and benefactress, who had just closed a life *sixty years* of which had been devoted to the poor of Celbridge and spent actually in their society, for very seldom was she more than three months out of the year away from Castletown, and often for years together without ever being three days away.

At last the melancholy morning came when her earthly remains were to be taken to their last home. As soon as daybreak appeared the people began to assemble in the park in front of the house, and by the time all was ready many thousands were assembled, for the *poor* came in numbers from every part of the county, and many from other counties also, thirty and forty miles off, so well was she known and so highly beloved and lamented. There is a great stone staircase leading up to the hall-door of Castletown House. Before these steps the multitude was collected, patiently and mournfully waiting to see the coffin come out.

I ordered the great door to be thrown open, and the procession moved from the hall towards the door. The moment the body appeared every hat was off, every eye intently fixed upon the coffin. One long, loud cry of despair issued from the assembled multitude. The next instant all was silent as death, and every being on their knees, their hands clasped in prayer, and their heads bowed in submission to the will of their Creator who had thought proper to strike this heavy blow. In this attitude all remained till the body reached the bottom of the steps, and the procession was again formed, the Duke of Leinster chief mourner, accompanied by my brothers and myself, and all the gentry for miles round, the coffin borne by her own labourers, who had begged 'I would not let her be placed in a hearse, but carried on the *shoulders* of those whom she *supported* in her life, and who would willingly have sacrificed theirs to preserve hers.'

Upon the word to move forward the people rose from their knees; again issued forth that one loud cry of grief, and we moved on without noise or wailing except from the sobs of the women (this being so contrary to the custom of the Irish it made a deep impression on us all). When the clergyman met us at the church door and commenced the burial service, again the hats were off, and this Catholic multitude were on their knees in fervent sincere prayer for the soul of their Protestant friend. We had then to proceed a long way through the town to the old ruined church where the family vault was, a deep silence continuing the whole way; and when arrived, and the coffin was lowered into the tomb, again that thrilling cry was heard, but louder and longer than ever, and a general rush was made to the vault, each striving to get a last look at the coffin which contained the remains of one they almost revered as a saint.

My poor sister had followed in a carriage, being determined to go down into the vault before it was closed and hid from her forever the being she most loved on earth. I thought it would be impossible, in the wretched state in which she was, to get her through the dense mass of people which obstructed the way from her carriage to the vault. However, the moment I said, 'My friends, here is my sister who wishes to go and see the last of her aunt; you all know her, and how they loved each other; I know how you pity and feel for her; pray make way for her to pass.'

The reply was, 'Oh, God! is it our dear Miss Emily? Oh, may the Great Father of mercy look down on you, you poor creature! Sure it's you that's to be pitied afore us all. Make way for the poor darling child of her we loved,' and in an instant all was silent, and a clear broad way opened for her to pass to the tomb, into which she descended. After some time I gently led her away, and ascending the steps, she again passed through the people, who had not moved but waited her return; and as she moved along leaning on my arm, her heart almost ready to burst with convulsive sobs, they tried to soothe and cheer her with every endearing expression of affection, and love, and gratitude, calling on her to remain with them and not leave Castletown; that they had only her left now, and if she left them what was to become of them?

In short, I never witnessed such sorrow, such gratitude, such respect, such a display of every kind feeling that is so conspicuous in the Irish peasant when called forth by the remembrance of kind and just treatment from those in affluence and above them in society. To be able to judge of Lady Louisa Conolly's character, and the reverence in which she was held by the whole of Ireland, it was necessary to have lived at Castletown during her life and to have witnessed her funeral after her death. She had been mistress of Castletown for sixty-five years, the whole of which long period was one continued scene of charity and benevolence. Her manners were truly noble; no affected condescension, but the plain simple sweetness that beamed in her fine countenance was reflected in her manners, and all derived their source from the same fountain of Christianity and meek humility which sprang spontaneously from her heart.

I never knew her equal; neither did I ever meet one who formed a clearer or sounder judgement on all difficult questions, or was more just in her perception of character. All the sentiments and views she has so often expressed to me, both of public occurrences and individual character and conduct, have been completely confirmed in every instance, and her perfect simplicity of religion and unbounded tolerance on that subject were extraordinary. With regard to affection for her friends and relations, it is only necessary to say that if misfortune, sorrow, or difficulty of any kind happened to any of them, Lady Louisa was at their side. Selfishness was what she had no idea of; I really do think she could not *understand* its meaning, so free was she from it; in short, I can only describe Lady Louisa Conolly's character by saying, that if it were possible (which it is not) to have the counterpart of Christ upon earth, she was His image.

Appendix

1

THE BURIAL OF SIR JOHN MOORE AFTER CORUÑA

Not a drum was heard, not a funeral note,
As his corse to the ramparts we hurried,
Not a soldier discharged his farewell shot
O'er the grave where our hero we buried.

We buried him darkly at dead of night,
The sods with our bayonets turning,
By the struggling moonbeam's misty light
And the lanterns dimly burning.

No useless coffin enclosed his breast,
Nor in sheet nor in shroud we wound him,
But he lay like a warrior taking his rest
With his martial cloak around him.

Few and short were the prayers we said,
And we spoke not a word of sorrow,
But we steadfastly gazed on the face of the dead.
And we bitterly thought of the morrow.

We thought, as we hollowed his narrow bed
And smoothed down his lonely pillow,
That the foe and the stranger would tread o'er his head,
And we far away on the billow.

Lightly they'll talk of the spirit that's gone,
And o'er his cold ashes upbraid him,
But little he'll reck if they let him sleep on
In the grave where his soldiers have laid him.

But half of our heavy task was done

When the bell tolled the hour for retiring,
And we learned by the distant and random gun
That the foe was suddenly firing.

Slowly and sadly we laid him down
From the field of his fame fresh and gory,
We carved not a line, we raised not a stone,
But we left him alone in his glory!—Charles Wolfe.
Trinity College, Dublin, 1817.

2

(Gallejos, January 21, 1812.
My dear Madam, I am sorry to tell you that your son, George, was again wounded in the right arm so badly last night, in the storm of Ciudad Rodrigo, as to make it necessary to amputate above the elbow. He, however, bore the operation remarkably well, and I have seen him this morning quite well, free from pain and fever, and enjoying highly his success before he had received his wound. When he did receive it he only desired that I might be told he had led his men to the top of the breach before he had fallen.

Having such sons, I am aware that you expect to hear of these misfortunes, which I have had more than once to communicate to you; and notwithstanding your affection for them, you have so just a notion of the value of the distinction which they are daily acquiring for themselves by their gallantry and good conduct, that their misfortunes do not make so great an impression upon you. Under these circumstances I perform the task I have taken on myself with less reluctance; hoping at the same time that this will be the last occasion on which I shall have to address you on such a subject, and that your brave sons will be spared to you.

Although the last was the most serious it was not the only wound which George received during the siege of Ciudad Rodrigo, he was hit by the splinter of a shell in the shoulder on the 16th.

Ever my dear Madam,
Yours most faithfully,
Wellington.

To Lady Sarah Napier.'

ALSO FROM LEONAUR
AVAILABLE IN SOFTCOVER OR HARDCOVER WITH DUST JACKET

THE RELUCTANT REBEL by *William G. Stevenson*—A young Kentuckian's experiences in the Confederate Infantry & Cavalry during the American Civil War..

BOOTS AND SADDLES by *Elizabeth B. Custer*—The experiences of General Custer's Wife on the Western Plains.

FANNIE BEERS' CIVIL WAR by *Fannie A. Beers*—A Confederate Lady's Experiences of Nursing During the Campaigns & Battles of the American Civil War.

LADY SALE'S AFGHANISTAN by *Florentia Sale*—An Indomitable Victorian Lady's Account of the Retreat from Kabul During the First Afghan War.

THE TWO WARS OF MRS DUBERLY by *Frances Isabella Duberly*—An Intrepid Victorian Lady's Experience of the Crimea and Indian Mutiny.

THE REBELLIOUS DUCHESS by *Paul F. S. Dermoncourt*—The Adventures of the Duchess of Berri and Her Attempt to Overthrow French Monarchy.

LADIES OF WATERLOO by *Charlotte A. Eaton, Magdalene de Lancey & Juana Smith*—The Experiences of Three Women During the Campaign of 1815: Waterloo Days by Charlotte A. Eaton, A Week at Waterloo by Magdalene de Lancey & Juana's Story by Juana Smith.

TWO YEARS BEFORE THE MAST by *Richard Henry Dana. Jr.*—The account of one young man's experiences serving on board a sailing brig—the Penelope—bound for California, between the years 1834-36.

A SAILOR OF KING GEORGE by *Frederick Hoffman*—From Midshipman to Captain—Recollections of War at Sea in the Napoleonic Age 1793-1815.

LORDS OF THE SEA by *A. T. Mahan*—Great Captains of the Royal Navy During the Age of Sail.

COGGESHALL'S VOYAGES: VOLUME 1 by *George Coggeshall*—The Recollections of an American Schooner Captain.

COGGESHALL'S VOYAGES: VOLUME 2 by *George Coggeshall*—The Recollections of an American Schooner Captain.

TWILIGHT OF EMPIRE by *Sir Thomas Ussher & Sir George Cockburn*—Two accounts of Napoleon's Journeys in Exile to Elba and St. Helena: Narrative of Events by Sir Thomas Ussher & Napoleon's Last Voyage: Extract of a diary by Sir George Cockburn.

AVAILABLE ONLINE AT **www.leonaur.com**
AND FROM ALL GOOD BOOK STORES

ALSO FROM LEONAUR
AVAILABLE IN SOFTCOVER OR HARDCOVER WITH DUST JACKET

IRON TIMES WITH THE GUARDS *by An O. E. (G. P. A. Fildes)*—The Experiences of an Officer of the Coldstream Guards on the Western Front During the First World War.

THE GREAT WAR IN THE MIDDLE EAST: 1 *by W. T. Massey*—The Desert Campaigns & How Jerusalem Was Won---two classic accounts in one volume.

THE GREAT WAR IN THE MIDDLE EAST: 2 *by W. T. Massey*—Allenby's Final Triumph.

SMITH-DORRIEN *by Horace Smith-Dorrien*—Isandlwhana to the Great War.

1914 *by Sir John French*—The Early Campaigns of the Great War by the British Commander.

GRENADIER *by E. R. M. Fryer*—The Recollections of an Officer of the Grenadier Guards throughout the Great War on the Western Front.

BATTLE, CAPTURE & ESCAPE *by George Pearson*—The Experiences of a Canadian Light Infantryman During the Great War.

DIGGERS AT WAR *by R. Hugh Knyvett & G. P. Cuttriss*—"Over There" With the Australians by R. Hugh Knyvett and Over the Top With the Third Australian Division by G. P. Cuttriss. Accounts of Australians During the Great War in the Middle East, at Gallipoli and on the Western Front.

HEAVY FIGHTING BEFORE US *by George Brenton Laurie*—The Letters of an Officer of the Royal Irish Rifles on the Western Front During the Great War.

THE CAMELIERS *by Oliver Hogue*—A Classic Account of the Australians of the Imperial Camel Corps During the First World War in the Middle East.

RED DUST *by Donald Black*—A Classic Account of Australian Light Horsemen in Palestine During the First World War.

THE LEAN, BROWN MEN *by Angus Buchanan*—Experiences in East Africa During the Great War with the 25th Royal Fusiliers—the Legion of Frontiersmen.

THE NIGERIAN REGIMENT IN EAST AFRICA *by W. D. Downes*—On Campaign During the Great War 1916-1918.

THE 'DIE-HARDS' IN SIBERIA *by John Ward*—With the Middlesex Regiment Against the Bolsheviks 1918-19.

AVAILABLE ONLINE AT **www.leonaur.com**
AND FROM ALL GOOD BOOK STORES

ALSO FROM LEONAUR
AVAILABLE IN SOFTCOVER OR HARDCOVER WITH DUST JACKET

THE ART OF WAR by Antoine Henri Jomini—Strategy & Tactics From the Age of Horse & Musket

THE MILITARY RELIGIOUS ORDERS OF THE MIDDLE AGES by F. C. Woodhouse—The Knights Templar, Hospitaller and Others.

THE BENGAL NATIVE ARMY by F. G. Cardew—An Invaluable Reference Resource.

THE 7TH (QUEEN'S OWN) HUSSARS: Volume 4—1688-1914 by C. R. B. Barrett—Uniforms, Equipment, Weapons, Traditions, the Services of Notable Officers and Men & the Appendices to All Volumes—Volume 4: 1688-1914.

THE SWORD OF THE CROWN by Eric W. Sheppard—A History of the British Army to 1914.

THE 7TH (QUEEN'S OWN) HUSSARS: Volume 3—1818-1914 by C. R. B. Barrett—On Campaign During the Canadian Rebellion, the Indian Mutiny, the Sudan, Matabeleland, Mashonaland and the Boer War Volume 3: 1818-1914.

THE CAMPAIGN OF WATERLOO by Antoine Henri Jomini—A Political & Military History from the French perspective.

THE AUXILIA OF THE ROMAN IMPERIAL ARMY by G. L. Cheeseman.

CAVALRY IN THE FRANCO-PRUSSIAN WAR by Jean Jacques Théophile Bonie & Otto August Johannes Kaehler—Actions of French Cavalry 1870 by Jean Jacques Théophile Bonie and Cavalry at Vionville & Mars-la-Tour by Otto August Johannes Kaehler.

NAPOLEON'S MEN AND METHODS by Alexander L. Kielland—The Rise and Fall of the Emperor and His Men Who Fought by His Side.

THE WOMAN IN BATTLE by Loreta Janeta Velazquez—Soldier, Spy and Secret Service Agent for the Confederancy During the American Civil War.

THE MILITARY SYSTEM OF THE ROMANS by Albert Harkness.

THE BATTLE OF ORISKANY 1777 by Ellis H. Roberts—The Conflict for the Mowhawk Valley During the American War of Independenc.

PERSONAL RECOLLECTIONS OF JOAN OF ARC by Mark Twain.

AVAILABLE ONLINE AT www.leonaur.com
AND FROM ALL GOOD BOOK STORES

www.ingramcontent.com/pod-product-compliance
Lightning Source LLC
Chambersburg PA
CBHW021005090426
42738CB00007B/656